Alfred,
Lord Tennyson

Selected and edited by MICHAEL BARON

University of London

WEIDENFELD & NICOLSON

This edition first published by Everyman Paperbacks in 1996

Introduction and other critical apparatus © J. M. Dent 1996

This edition published in 2022 by Weidenfeld & Nicolson
An imprint of The Orion Publishing Group Ltd
Carmelite House
50 Victoria Embankment
London EC4Y 0DZ

An Hachette UK Company

1 3 5 7 9 10 8 6 4 2

A CIP catalogue record for this book
is available from the British Library.

ISBN (mmp) 978 1 4746 2593 7
ISBN (ebook) 978 1 7802 2342 1

Printed in the UK by Clays Ltd, Elcograf S.p.A.

www.orionbooks.co.uk
www.weidenfeldandnicolson.co.uk

Contents

Note on the Author and Editor

ALFRED TENNYSON was born in Somersby in the Lincolnshire Wolds on 6 August 1809, fourth son of the rector in a family of eleven surviving children. At Trinity College, Cambridge, he met Arthur Hallam, who became his close friend, and whose early death in 1833 is reflected in a number of his poems, chiefly *In Memoriam* (1850). His first independent volume, *Poems, Chiefly Lyrical*, was published in 1830; the next, *Poems* (1833), contained some of his most celebrated poems and he was deeply hurt by the vehemence of antagonistic reviews. They were much revised for his next collection, *Poems* (1842), which established him as the foremost poet of the age. Before this his family had moved from Lincolnshire to Essex, and he had become engaged to Emily Sellwood. The engagement was broken off in 1840 partly because of his anxiety about his health and his financial prospects as a man committed to writing poetry. He lost his capital through a bad investment in 1843 and suffered an emotional breakdown in the following year. In 1850 he published *In Memoriam*, married Emily Sellwood and succeeded Wordsworth as Poet Laureate. *Maud* appeared in 1855; it was criticised as morbid and obscure, but a century later it was seen as central to Tennyson's work. The first four parts of *Idylls of the King* appeared in 1859, and it was completed in 1885. He entered the House of Lords as Baron Tennyson in March 1884, and after his death in October 1892 was given a public funeral in Westminster Abbey.

MICHAEL BARON is Senior Lecturer at Birkbeck College, University of London. His publications include *Language and Relationship in Wordsworth's Writing* (1995), an edition of T. L. Peacock's *Headlong Hall* and *Gryll Grange* and articles on Romantic and post-Romantic poetry. Until 1994 he was co-editor of *English*.

Chronology of Tennyson's Life

Year	Life
1809	(6 August) Born at Somersby, Lincolnshire, fourth son of the rector George Tennyson and Elizabeth Fytehe
1815	Attends Louth Grammar School
1820	Leaves Louth to be educated at home by his father
1824	Father suffers mental and physical breakdown

Chronology of his Times

Year	Literary Context	Historical Events
1809	*Quarterly Review* founded	
1812	Crabbe, *Tales* Byron, *Childe Harold's Pilgrimage*	Napoleon invades Russia
1813	Austen, *Pride and Prejudice*	
1814	Austen, *Mansfield Park* Wordsworth, *The Excursion* Scott, *Waverley*	Wellington enters Madrid. Napoleon abdicates
1815	Wordsworth, *Poems*	
1817	*Blackwood's Edinburgh Magazine* founded	
1818	Austen, *Northanger Abbey* and *Persuasion* Keats, *Endymion* M. Shelley, *Frankenstein*	
1819	Shelley, *The Cenci* Crabbe, *Tales of the Hall* Byron, *Don Juan, I–II*	Birth of Queen Victoria
1820	Shelley, *Prometheus Unbound* Keats, *Poems* Scott, *Ivanhoe*	Prince Regent succeeds as George IV. Congress of Vienna
1821	Byron, *Don Juan, III–V, Cain* De Quincey, *Confessions of an English Opium Eater*	Greek War of Independence begins
1824	*Westminster Review* founded	

Year	Life
1827	*Poems by Two Brothers* with Charles and Edward. Enters Trinity College, Cambridge
1829	Friendship with Arthur Hallam begins. Member of the Apostles, an undergraduate society at Cambridge. Wins Chancellor's Gold Medal with prize poem 'Timbuctoo'
1830	*Poems, Chiefly Lyrical*. Visits the Pyrenees with Hallam
1831	Father dies (March). Leaves Cambridge without taking a degree. Hallam reviews *Poems, Chiefly Lyrical*
1832	*Poems* (dated 1833 on title page and usually referred to as *Poems 1833*). Edward Tennyson becomes insane
1833	Hallam becomes engaged to Emily Tennyson (spring); dies (September)
1834	Falls in love with Rosa Baring
1837	Family moves to High Beech, Epping. Family recognises engagement to Emily Sellwood
1840	Engagement broken off. Family moves to Tunbridge Wells, then Boxley (Kent)
1842	*Poems* (enlarged edition in two volumes)
1843	Loses his entire fortune after investing in a wood-carving business
1844	Emotional breakdown

Year	Literary Context	Historical Events
1828		Wellington becomes Prime Minister
1829		Catholic Emancipation Act
1830	Lyell, *Principles of Geology*, vol 1 Cobbett, *Rural Rides*	George IV dies; William IV succeeds. July Revolution in France
1832		First Reform Act
1833	Browning, *Pauline* Carlyle, *Sartor Resartus*	Abolition of slavery
1834		New Poor Law. Burning of the Houses of Parliament. Tolpuddle Martyrs
1836	Dickens, *Pickwick Papers*	Conclusion of Darwin's *Beagle* voyage
1837	Dickens, *Oliver Twist* Carlyle, *The French Revolution*	William IV dies; Victoria succeeds
1838	Dickens, *Nicholas Nickleby*	Chartist movement begins
1840	Dickens, *The Old Curiosity Shop* Browning, *Sordello*	Victoria marries Prince Albert
1842	Browning, *Dramatic Lyrics*	Chartist riots
1843	Dickens, *A Christmas Carol* Wordsworth made Poet Laureate	
1844	Dickens, *Martin Chuzzlewit* Carlyle, *Past and Present*	Newman becomes a Roman Catholic

Year	Life
1845	Receives Civil List pension (£200 per annum)
1847	*The Princess*
1849	Renews correspondence with Emily Sellwood
1850	*In Memoriam* published anonymously (May). Marries Emily Sellwood (June). Appointed Poet Laureate (November), succeeding Wordsworth
1851	Visits Italy with Emily
1852	Son, Hallam, born. 'Ode on the Death of the Duke of Wellington'
1853	Moves to Farringford, Isle of Wight
1854	Son, Lionel, born
1855	*Maud, and Other Poems*

Year	Literary Context	Historical Events
1845	Browning, *Dramatic Romances and Lyrics*	Co-operative movement founded
1846		Irish potato famine. Repeal of Corn Laws
1847	Thackeray, *Vanity Fair*	California gold rush begins. Ten Hours Factory Act
1848	Marx and Engels, *The Communist Manifesto* Dickens, *Dombey and Son* Clough, *The Bothie of Tober-na-Vuolich* Gaskell, *Mary Barton*	Revolutions in Europe. Louis Napoleon elected President of France. Roman Republic. Chartist demonstrations in London
1849	Dickens, *David Copperfield* Thackeray, *Pendennis* Arnold, *The Strayed Reveller*	
1850	E. B. Browning, *Sonnets from the Portuguese*	Re-establishment of Catholic hierarchy in England.
1851	Ruskin, *The Stones of Venice*	Great Exhibition. Napoleon III becomes Emperor of France
1852	Dickens, *Bleak House* Thackeray, *Henry Esmond*	Death of Wellington
1853	Arnold, *Poems* Gaskell, *Ruth* and *Cranford*	
1854	Dickens, *Hard Times*	Crimean War begins. Working Man's College opens
1855	Browning, *Men and Women* Dickens, *Little Dorrit* Trollope, *The Warden*	Sebastopol falls
1856		End of Crimean War. Victoria Cross instituted. British war with China begins

Year	Life
1859	*Idylls of the King* published (four parts)
1860	Helps F. T. Palgrave to compile the anthology *The Golden Treasury*
1862	New edition of *Idylls*, dedicated to the memory of Prince Albert. First audience with Queen Victoria
1864	Garibaldi visits the Tennysons at Farringford. *Enoch Arden and Other Poems*

Year	Literary Context	Historical Events
1857	Eliot, *Scenes of Clerical Life* Trollope, *Barchester Towers* E. B. Browning, *Aurora Leigh*	Indian Mutiny begins
1858	Clough, *Amours de Voyage*	Government of India transferred to Britain
1859	Darwin, *The Origin of Species* Dickins, *A Tale of Two Cities* Eliot, *Adam Bede*	
1860	Collins, *The Woman in White* Eliot, *The Mill on the Floss*	Unification of Italy
1861	Dickens, *Great Expectations* Eliot, *Silas Marner* Trollope, *Framley Parsonage*	American Civil War begins. Death of Prince Albert
1862	Eliot, *Romola* Meredith, *Modern Love*	
1863	Gaskell, *Sylvia's Lovers*	
1864	Browning, *Dramatis Personae* Dickens, *Our Mutual Friend* Gaskell, *Wives and Daughters*	
1865	Arnold, *Essays in Criticism* Carroll, *Alice in Wonderland*	American Civil War ends. Lincoln assassinated
1867	Marx, *Capital*, vol 1 Arnold, *New Poems; On the Study of Celtic Literature*	Second Reform Act

Year	Life
1869	*The Holy Grail and Other Poems*
1872	*Gareth and Lynette*
1875	*Queen Mary* (play; produced at Lyceum Theatre, London, 1876)
1876	*Harold* (play)
1878	Son, Lionel, marries Eleanor Locker
1879	Death of brother, Charles Tennyson Turner. *The Falcon* (play) produced
1880	*Ballads and Other Poems*
1881	*The Cup* (play) produced by Henry Irving
1882	*The Promise of May* (play in prose) produced
1883	Accepts barony
1884	*The Cup and The Falcon*. Son, Hallam, marries Audrey Boyle. *Becket* (play)
1885	*Balin and Balan* and *Tiresias and Other Poems*
1886	Son, Lionel, dies. *Locksley Hall Sixty Years After*

Year	Literary Context	Historical Events
	Trollope, *Last Chronicles of Barset*	
1868	Browning, *The Ring and the Book* Collins, *The Moonstone*	Gladstone replaces Disraeli as Prime Minister. First Meeting of the Trades Union Congress
1869	Arnold, *Culture and Anarchy*	Opening of Suez Canal
1870	Rossetti, *Poems* Dickens, *Edwin Drood*	Franco-Prussian War. Married Woman's Property Act
1871	Darwin, *The Descent of Man* Eliot, *Middlemarch*	Paris Commune. Trade unions legalised in Britain
1872	Hardy, *Under the Greenwood Tree* Carroll, *Through the Looking Glass*	Civil War in Spain
1874	Hardy, *Far From the Madding Crowd*	Disraeli becomes Prime Minister
1875		Britain gains control of the Suez Canal
1876	Eliot, *Daniel Deronda*	Victoria becomes Empress of India
1878	Hardy, *The Return of the Native*	Congress of Berlin
1879	Meredith, *The Egoist*	
1880	Hardy, *The Trumpet Major*	
1881	Hardy, *A Laodicean*	
1882	Hardy, *Two on a Tower*	First Boer War ends
1883	Stevenson, *Treasure Island*	
1884		Third Reform Bill
1885	Pater, *Marius the Epicurean*	
1886	Stevenson, *Dr Jekyll and Mr Hyde* Hardy, *The Mayor of Casterbridge*	Irish Home Rule Bill introduced by Gladstone

Year	Life
1888	Suffers serious illness
1889	*Demeter and Other Poems*
1892	*The Forester* (play). *Becket* produced by Irving. Dies (6 October). *The Death of Oenone, Akbar's Dream, and Other Poems*

Year	Literary Context	Historical Events
1887	Hardy, *The Woodlanders*	Queen Victoria's Golden Jubilee
1888	Arnold, *Essays in Criticism (second series)*	Jack the Ripper murders in London
1889	Stevenson, *The Master of Ballantrae*	
1890	Wilde, *The Picture of Dorian Gray*	First underground railway in London
1891	Hardy, *Tess of the d'Urbervilles*	
1892	Wilde, *Lady Windermere's Fan* produced	

Introduction

When in 1884 Alfred Tennyson became Baron Tennyson of Aldworth and Freshwater, the only man ever to have been raised to the peerage solely because of his poetry, there were murmurs that 'The People's Poet' should not have accepted the honour: testament to the quite extraordinary social range of his admirers, from the Queen and the Prime Minister, Gladstone, to the 'cockneys' (as Tennyson called them) who gaped over his garden wall. Forty years earlier some of his poems had been set in the universities as texts for translation into Latin. He became a literary lion, like his great contemporary Dickens, and was famous for reciting his poems tirelessly to private audiences. They wept when he read 'Guinevere', a contemporary favourite; even people who were by no means uncritical wept, people such as George Eliot, who had attacked *Maud* in a review – which Tennyson seems not to have read. He was Poet Laureate for two-thirds of Victoria's long reign.

If this suggests a man at home with his era, it is at most half true: his poems were sometimes found morbid, unhealthy, obsessive or unmanly in their exploration of personal and national identity, and of scepticism about religion, science and history. For modern readers poems such as 'Locksley Hall', 'The Golden Year', *In Memoriam* and *Maud* appeal because these subject matters are of perennial interest, but also because there is a special determination and touchiness in Tennyson's treatment of them (hence, perhaps, the reviewers' comments), a quality that tells us much about Victorian preoccupations with health, manliness and empire.

Tennyson's first intellectual milieu was Trinity College, Cambridge, which he entered in 1827, and the death six years later of his Cambridge friend and fellow poet Arthur Hallam affected his life and his writing deeply, not only in the elegiac sequence *In Memoriam* but also in a number of earlier poems, including 'Morte d'Arthur' and 'Ulysses', and an early version of 'Tithonus'; poems about friendship, loss, isolation and survival. Hallam's role was philosophical as well as personal: his review of *Poems, Chiefly Lyrical* in 1831 defined a new kind of poetry, a poetry of sensation and observation rather than moral reflection. These ideas had clearly been discussed with Tennyson himself, and they do much to define the preoccupation with beauty and art in early poems such as 'The Palace of Art' and 'The Lady of Shalott', which is quite different from the emphasis on moral strength that we find in Matthew Arnold's work and that we sometimes think of as quintessentially Victorian. Hallam's essay remained influential, and sixty years later W. B. Yeats, who was deeply antagonistic to the moral strain in Victorian poetry, thought of it as a precursor of his own early (symbolist) theories, in which he reacted againt 'the moral law' and 'scientific opinion' as subject matter for poetry.

But we should not read into Tennyson's poems a simple opposition between the moral and the aesthetic, especially if that implies an aloofness from contemporary life and thought. As a matter of fact he *was* criticised for writing musical but empty verses (especially a group of poems about young women: 'Lilian', 'Adeline', 'Claribel', and others) and for using remote material in *Idylls of the King*, but recent revaluations of his major poetry – Isobel Armstrong's in *Victorian Poetry: Poetry, Poetics and Politics*, for example – have shown how deeply its language is embedded in social and political debate, whatever the ostensible subject matter. Some poems are indeed about withdrawal from the social to the personal and from the personal to the social – 'Locksley Hall', *In Memoriam* and *Maud* are strikingly varied examples – but he imagines these realms in terms that have distinct contemporary resonance.

In Memoriam is about personal love and loss and is one of the great poems of friendship, because the speaker imagines himself as brother, spouse, lover and mother of his dead friend, and looks for words to give a reality to the complex of feelings and duties Hallam's name and memory evoke. Like all elegies it imagines ways of thinking about the future as well as the past in order to see loss as part of a pattern of meaning, and the speaker is tempted to equate loss with evil and religious consolation with good ('Oh yet we hope that somehow good/Will be the final goal of ill'). Reading the poem this way we can construct a narrative of loss and reconciliation organised around the three Christmas scenes that punctuate it (see sections 105–6 and notes, below), a movement from grief to doubt to faith. But there are broader perspectives. Brooding over the earth in which the dead are buried, the speaker questions in what sense even nature and the human race survive. It isn't just that nature is 'red in tooth and claw' (Tennyson was sensitive to the scientific ethos in which Darwin wrote *The Origin of Species*), but that the future is imagined in terms of geological changes, such as those described in Charles Lyell's *Principles of Geology*. Thoughts of spiritual survival may conflict with the amoral and perhaps incomprehensible processes of global change. It is the wrestling with these ideas, almost as if they were personal antagonists, that makes the poem a uniquely powerful exploration of both subjective time (memory and hope) and the history of the human race, however much it is specific to its own time and place.

Tennyson described *Maud*, the poem now considered his most distinctive, in these terms:

> a little *Hamlet*, the history of a morbid, poetic soul, under the blighting influence of a recklessly speculative age. He is the heir of madness, an egoist with the makings of a cynic, raised to a pure and holy love which elevates his whole nature, passing from the height of triumph to the lowest depth of misery, driven into madness by the loss of her whom he has loved, and, when he has at length passed through the fiery furnace, and has recovered his reason, giving himself up to work for the good of mankind through the unselfishness born of a great passion.

He strikingly reinterprets Shakespeare's play as an argument against materialism or 'mammonism' as it was called in the mid-nineteenth century and indicates, without quite saying so, that a young man's sexual desires and ambition to rise socially might be sublimated, refined and simplified, in the service of the nation – in this case by enlisting as a soldier in the Crimean War. In the previous year Tennyson had lamented the soldiers who died in one of the more newsworthy episodes of the war, the charge of the Light Brigade at Balaclava. Should we see the protagonist in *Maud* as having come to his senses at the end of the poem or as still deluded, substituting one kind of moral irresponsibility for another? Tennyson had experienced family division (his grandfather virtually disinherited his father, who became mentally unstable), and had a long-standing fear of epilepsy and narcotic addiction (some members of his family suffered in these ways), and these clearly played a part in creating the circumstances of the poem. So perhaps did his disastrous investment in Matthew Allen's scheme to make wood-carvings using steam power; Allen was proprietor of an asylum Tennyson visited in 1837–41 and author of *Essay on the Classification of the Insane* (1837). But we should not assume that the protagonist's conclusions are Tennyson's, and in any case, what is important is that the poem expresses forms of self-division that are shaped by specific social abuses and pressures. One of the pleasures of reading *Maud* is discovering that where it is modern, it is also distinctively of its time.

Tennyson said that 'the peculiarity of this poem is that different phases of passion in one person take the place of different characters'. In this sense the poem is dramatic, a prime example of what Matthew Arnold in 1853 stigmatised as 'the mind's dialogue with itself', a sign of the decadence of modern poetry. Arnold valued poetry of formal beauty and repose and was out of sympathy with experiments in introspection, but his phrase neatly identified a kind of modernity that appeals to twentieth-century readers, whether in Robert Browning's dramatic monologues or Tennyson's – poems such as 'Ulysses', 'Tithonus' and 'St Simeon Stylites'. Here Tennyson presents a historical or mythological figure reflecting on his circumstances but also revealing unconsciously a great deal more about himself, and the poems invite us to read them with an awareness of this irony and even with humour. The dialect poem 'Northern Farmer, New Style' can be seen in a similar way, except that here the humour is more conventionally satiric as Tennyson addresses one of his favourite contemporary themes, avarice and social climbing.

He returned to the past in his most expansive project, *Idylls of the King*. He had brooded since boyhood on the Arthurian subject matter, but his first published lines on it, the 'Morte d'Arthur', were, like the lyrics of *In Memoriam*, a response to Arthur Hallam's premature death. Loss and transience remained at the centre of the project. Many of his contemporaries found the material disappointingly remote from contemporary life, and it is easy to see how the accumulating sequence of tales seemed a withdrawal from the anguished topicality of parts of *Maud*. Could this be the great work of the Poet Laureate in the age of empire? Like *In Memoriam*, *Idylls* is a collection of poems written over many years and gradually shaped into a whole. But unlike *In Memoriam* it is clearly intended to have a strong narrative unity, and critics have debated how far this is achieved. It has the size and the subject matter of an epic poem – the fall of a civilisation – but it tends to remain a series of episodes in which the narrative element is slight and the descriptive, the pictorial element correspondingly strong. It is true that he had a great gift for visual and aural effects, as the stately 'Morte d'Arthur' shows, and little gift for fast-moving narrative or dramatic conflict between characters (the stage plays he wrote in the late 1870s and 1880s were unsuccessful and are now unread); but in reworking his Arthurian sources into a multi-layered exploration of love, loyalty, friendship, the exercise of personal power and the place of morality in politics, he produced a rich and disturbing poem. The breakdown of values forms the broad subject matter of the *Idylls*, and Tennyson handles it with a range and virtuosity that cannot be summed up as mere pictorialism. The central event, Guinevere's betrayal of King Arthur, is mirrored in Vivien's seduction of the magician Merlin, but these are presented in very different kinds of poetry, the former chiefly in Arthur's lengthy complaint (in 'Guinevere'), which strikes a sentimental note and was a favourite with Tennyson's contemporaries, the latter in some powerfully erotic writing (included in this edition) that offended some readers. Merlin's vanity, self-deception and defensive priggishness are no less remarkably presented than Vivien's resourceful duplicity, and this focus on the complexities of desire and self-esteem surely undermines any general notion that the poem is simply, as Tennyson put it, about the war between 'spirit and flesh'. These narratives, again like *In Memoriam*, reveal much about Victorian views of the masculine and the feminine.

I have emphasised poems in which Tennyson and his protagonists are solitary, even isolated figures, but he wrote a great many poems of a more domestic or companionable nature, including a series of 'English Idylls', immensely popular with his contemporaries but now little regarded. It may be that we are unable to value them properly because our own official notions of family and community ('Victorian values'?) are still too close to theirs. At all events some of his shorter pieces speak intimately, including the verse-letter to Edward FitzGerald and the lyric 'June Bracken and Heather' which Tennyson addressed to his wife in old age. This poem makes an excellent contrast with the much more famous 'Crossing the Bar', and since it was written later, I have gone against convention and printed it last.

In making this short selection of Tennyson's poems, I have chosen complete texts wherever possible. Neither *In Memoriam* nor

Idylls of the King could be included whole, and I regret it has been necessary to select from *Maud* as well. I have also excerpted the 'Ode on the Death of the Duke of Wellington', which seems to me over-long, the central sections falling far short of the beginning and end in rhetorical power. The passages selected, along with 'The Charge of the Light Brigade', give a good sample of Tennyson's rare ability to write memorable public poetry.

MICHAEL BARON

Alfred, Lord Tennyson

The Outcast

I will not seek my Father's groves,
They murmur deeply o'er my head
Of sunless days and broken loves:
Their shade is dim and dark and dead.
There through the length of cool arcades
Where noonday leaves the midnight dews,
Unreal shapes of twilight shades
Along the sombre avenues,
To Memory's widowed eyes would spring
In dreamy, drowsy wandering.   10

I will not seek my Father's hills,
Their hue is fresh and clear and bright,
What time the early sunbeam fills
Their bush-clad depths with lonely light.
Each broken stile, each wavy path,
Each hollowed hawthorn, damp, and black,
Each brook that chatters noisy wrath
Among its knotted reeds, bring back
Lone images of varied pain
To this worn mind and fevered brain.   20

I will not seek my Father's Hall:
There peers the day's unhallowed glare,
The wet moss crusts the parting wall,
The wassail wind is reveller there.
Along the weedy, chinky floors
Wild knots of flowering rushes blow
And through the sounding corridors
The sere leaf rustles to and fro:
And O! what Memory might recall,
If once I paced that voiceless Hall!   30

Mariana

'Mariana in the moated grange.'
Measure for Measure

With blackest moss the flower-plots
   Were thickly crusted, one and all:
The rusted nails fell from the knots
   That held the pear to the gable-wall.
The broken sheds look'd sad and strange:
   Unlifted was the clinking latch;
   Weeded and worn the ancient thatch
Upon the lonely moated grange.
      She only said, 'My life is dreary,
         He cometh not,' she said;   10
      She said, 'I am aweary, aweary,
         I would that I were dead!'

Her tears fell with the dews at even;
   Her tears fell ere the dews were dried;
She could not look on the sweet heaven,
   Either at morn or eventide.
After the flitting of the bats,
   When thickest dark did trance the sky,
   She drew her casement-curtain by,
And glanced athwart the glooming flats.   20
      She only said, 'The night is dreary,
         He cometh not,' she said;
      She said, 'I am aweary, aweary,
         I would that I were dead!'

Upon the middle of the night,
   Waking she heard the night-fowl crow:
The cock sung out an hour ere light:
   From the dark fen the oxen's low
Came to her: without hope of change,
   In sleep she seem'd to walk forlorn,   30
   Till cold winds woke the gray-eyed morn
About the lonely moated grange.

She only said, 'The day is dreary,
　　He cometh not,' she said;
She said, 'I am aweary, aweary,
　　I would that I were dead!'

About a stone-cast from the wall
　A sluice with blacken'd waters slept,
And o'er it many, round and small,
　The cluster'd marish-mosses crept.
Hard by a poplar shook alway,
　All silver-green with gnarled bark:
For leagues no other tree did mark
The level waste, the rounding gray.
　　She only said, 'My life is dreary,
　　He cometh not,' she said;
　　She said, 'I am aweary, aweary,
　　　I would that I were dead!'

And ever when the moon was low,
　And the shrill winds were up and away,
In the white curtain, to and fro,
　She saw the gusty shadow sway.
But when the moon was very low,
　And wild winds bound within their cell,
　The shadow of the poplar fell
Upon her bed, across her brow.
　　She only said, 'The night is dreary,
　　He cometh not,' she said;
　　She said, 'I am aweary, aweary,
　　　I would that I were dead!'

All day within the dreamy house,
　The doors upon their hinges creak'd;
The blue fly sung in the pane; the mouse
　Behind the mouldering wainscot shriek'd,
Or from the crevice peer'd about.
　Old faces glimmer'd thro' the doors,
　Old footsteps trod the upper floors,
Old voices called her from without.
　　She only said, 'My life is dreary,

He cometh not,' she said;   70
She said, 'I am aweary, aweary,
I would that I were dead!'

The sparrow's chirrup on the roof,
The slow clock ticking, and the sound
Which to the wooing wind aloof
The poplar made, did all confound
Her sense; but most she loathed the hour
When the thick-moted sunbeam lay
Athwart the chambers, and the day
Was sloping toward his western bower,   80
Then, said she, 'I am very dreary,
He will not come,' she said;
She wept, 'I am aweary, aweary,
Oh God, that I were dead!'

The Lady of Shalott

PART 1

On either side the river lie
Long fields of barley and of rye,
That clothe the wold and meet the sky;
And thro' the field the road runs by
To many-tower'd Camelot;
And up and down the people go,
Gazing where the lilies blow
Round an island there below,
The island of Shalott.

Willows whiten, aspens quiver,   10
Little breezes dusk and shiver
Thro' the wave that runs for ever
By the island in the river
Flowing down to Camelot.

Four gray walls, and four gray towers,
Overlook a space of flowers,
And the silent isle imbowers
    The Lady of Shalott.

By the margin, willow-veil'd,
Slide the heavy barges trail'd   20
By slow horses; and unhail'd
The shallop flitteth silken-sail'd
    Skimming down to Camelot:
But who hath seen her wave her hand?
Or at the casement seen her stand?
Or is she known in all the land,
    The Lady of Shalott?

Only reapers, reaping early
In among the bearded barley,
Hear a song that echoes cheerly   30
From the river winding clearly
    Down to tower'd Camelot:
And by the moon the reaper weary,
Piling sheaves in uplands airy,
Listening, whispers ''Tis the fairy
    Lady of Shalott.'

PART 2

There she weaves by night and day
A magic web with colours gay.
She has heard a whisper say,
A curse is on her if she stay   40
    To look down to Camelot.
She knows not what the curse may be,
And so she weaveth steadily,
And little other care hath she,
    The Lady of Shalott.

And moving thro' a mirror clear
That hangs before her all the year,

Shadows of the world appear.
There she sees the highway near
    Winding down to Camelot: 50
There the river eddy whirls,
And there the surly village-churls,
And the red cloaks of market girls,
    Pass onward from Shalott.

Sometimes a troop of damsels glad,
An abbot on an ambling pad,
Sometimes a curly shepherd-lad,
Or long-hair'd page in crimson clad,
    Goes by to tower'd Camelot;
And sometimes thro' the mirror blue   60
The knights come riding two and two:
She hath no loyal knight and true,
    The Lady of Shalott.

But in her web she still delights
To weave the mirror's magic sights,
For often thro' the silent nights
A funeral, with plumes and lights
    And music, went to Camelot:
Or when the moon was overhead,
Came two young lovers lately wed;   70
'I am half sick of shadows,' said
    The Lady of Shalott.

PART 3

A bow-shot from her bower-eaves,
He rode between the barley-sheaves,
The sun came dazzling thro' the leaves,
And flamed upon the brazen greaves
    Of bold Sir Lancelot.
A red-cross knight for ever kneel'd
To a lady in his shield,
That sparkled on the yellow field,   80
    Beside remote Shalott.

The gemmy bridle glitter'd free,
Like to some branch of stars we see
Hung in the golden Galaxy.
The bridle bells rang merrily
      As he rode down to Camelot:
And from his blazon'd baldric slung
A mighty silver bugle hung,
And as he rode his armour rung,
      Beside remote Shalott.   90

All in the blue unclouded weather
Thick-jewell'd shone the saddle-leather,
The helmet and the helmet-feather
Burn'd like one burning flame together,
      As he rode down to Camelot.
As often thro' the purple night,
Below the starry clusters bright,
Some bearded meteor, trailing light,
      Moves over still Shalott.

His broad clear brow in sunlight glow'd;   100
On burnished hooves his war-horse trode;
From underneath his helmet flow'd
His coal-black curls as on he rode,
      As he rode down to Camelot.
From the bank and from the river
He flash'd into the crystal mirror,
'Tirra lirra,' by the river
      Sang Sir Lancelot.

She left the web, she left the loom,
She made three paces thro' the room,   110
She saw the water-lily bloom,
She saw the helmet and the plume,
      She look'd down to Camelot.
Out flew the web and floated wide;
The mirror crack'd from side to side;
'The curse is come upon me,' cried
      The Lady of Shalott.

PART 4

In the stormy east-wind straining,
The pale yellow woods were waning,
The broad stream in his banks complaining,   120
Heavily the low sky raining
  Over tower'd Camelot;
Down she came and found a boat
Beneath a willow left afloat,
And round about the prow she wrote
  The Lady of Shalott.

And down the river's dim expanse
Like some bold seër in a trance,
Seeing all his own mischance –
With a glassy countenance   130
  Did she look to Camelot.
And at the closing of the day
She loosed the chain, and down she lay;
The broad stream bore her far away,
  The Lady of Shalott.

Lying, robed in snowy white
That loosely flew to left and right –
The leaves upon her falling light –
Thro' the noises of the night
  She floated down to Camelot: 140
And as the boat-head wound along
The willowy hills and fields among,
They heard her singing her last song,
  The Lady of Shalott.

Heard a carol, mournful, holy,
Chanted loudly, chanted lowly,
Till her blood was frozen slowly,
And her eyes were darken'd wholly,
  Turn'd to tower'd Camelot.
For ere she reach'd upon the tide   150
The first house by the water-side,

Singing in her song she died,
    The Lady of Shalott.

Under tower and balcony,
By garden-wall and gallery,
A gleaming shape she floated by,
Dead-pale between the houses high,
    Silent into Camelot.
Out upon the wharfs they came,
Knight and burgher, lord and dame,   160
And round the prow they read her name,
    The Lady of Shalott.

Who is this? and what is here?
And in the lighted palace near
Died the sound of royal cheer;
And they cross'd themselves for fear,
    All the knights at Camelot:
But Lancelot mused a little space;
He said, 'She has a lovely face;
God in his mercy lend her grace,   170
    The Lady of Shalott.'

The Lotos-eaters

'Courage!' he said, and pointed toward the land,
'This mounting wave will roll us shoreward soon.'
In the afternoon they came unto a land
In which it seemed always afternoon.
All round the coast the languid air did swoon,
Breathing like one that hath a weary dream.
Full-faced above the valley stood the moon;
And like a downward smoke, the slender stream
Along the cliff to fall and pause and fall did seem.

A land of streams! some, like a downward smoke,   10
Slow-dropping veils of thinnest lawn, did go;

And some thro' wavering lights and shadows broke,
Rolling a slumbrous sheet of foam below.
They saw the gleaming river seaward flow
From the inner land: far off, three mountain-tops,
Three silent pinnacles of aged snow,
Stood sunset-flush'd: and, dew'd with showery drops,
Up-clomb the shadowy pine above the woven copse.

The charmed sunset linger'd low adown
In the red West: thro' mountain clefts the dale   20
Was seen far inland, and the yellow down
Border'd with palm, and many a winding vale
And meadow, set with slender galingale;
A land where all things always seem'd the same!
And round about the keel with faces pale,
Dark faces pale against that rosy flame,
The mild-eyed melancholy Lotos-eaters came.

Branches they bore of that enchanted stem,
Laden with flower and fruit, whereof they gave
To each, but whoso did receive of them,   30
And taste, to him the gushing of the wave
Far far away did seem to mourn and rave
On alien shores; and if his fellow spake,
His voice was thin, as voices from the grave;
And deep-asleep he seem'd, yet all awake,
And music in his ears his beating heart did make.

They sat them down upon the yellow sand,
Between the sun and moon upon the shore;
And sweet it was to dream of Fatherland,
Of child, and wife, and slave; but evermore   40
Most weary seem'd the sea, weary the oar,
Weary the wandering fields of barren foam.
Then some one said, 'We will return no more;'
And all at once they sang, 'Our island home
Is far beyond the wave; we will no longer roam.'

Ulysses

It little profits that an idle king,
By this still hearth, among these barren crags,
Match'd with an aged wife, I mete and dole
Unequal laws unto a savage race,
That hoard, and sleep, and feed, and know not me.
I cannot rest from travel: I will drink
Life to the lees: all times I have enjoy'd
Greatly, have suffer'd greatly, both with those
That loved me, and alone; on shore, and when
Thro' scudding drifts the rainy Hyades   10
Vext the dim sea: I am become a name;
For always roaming with a hungry heart
Much have I seen and known; cities of men
And manners, climates, councils, governments,
Myself not least, but honour'd of them all;
And drunk delight of battle with my peers,
Far on the ringing plains of windy Troy.
I am a part of all that I have met;
Yet all experience is an arch wherethro'
Gleams that untravell'd world, whose margin fades   20
For ever and for ever when I move.
How dull it is to pause, to make an end,
To rust unburnish'd, not to shine in use!
As tho' to breathe were life. Life piled on life
Were all too little, and of one to me
Little remains: but every hour is saved
From that eternal silence, something more,
A bringer of new things; and vile it were
For some three suns to store and hoard myself,
And this gray spirit yearning in desire   30
To follow knowledge like a sinking star,
Beyond the utmost bound of human thought.
    This is my son, mine own Telemachus,
To whom I leave the sceptre and the isle –
Well-loved of me, discerning to fulfil
This labour, by slow prudence to make mild
A rugged people, and thro' soft degrees

Subdue them to the useful and the good.
Most blameless is he, centred in the sphere
Of common duties, decent not to fail 40
In offices of tenderness, and pay
Meet adoration to my household gods,
When I am gone. He works his work, I mine.
There lies the port; the vessel puffs her sail:
There gloom the dark broad seas. My mariners,
Souls that have toil'd, and wrought, and thought with me –
That ever with a frolic welcome took
The thunder and the sunshine, and opposed
Free hearts, free foreheads – you and I are old;
Old age hath yet his honour and his toil; 50
Death closes all: but something ere the end,
Some work of noble note, may yet be done,
Not unbecoming men that strove with Gods.
The lights begin to twinkle from the rocks:
The long day wanes: the slow moon climbs: the deep
Moans round with many voices. Come, my friends,
'Tis not too late to seek a newer world.
Push off, and sitting well in order smite
The sounding furrows; for my purpose holds
To sail beyond the sunset, and the baths 60
Of all the western stars, until I die.
It may be that the gulfs will wash us down:
It may be we shall touch the Happy Isles,
And see the great Achilles, whom we knew.
Tho' much is taken, much abides; and tho'
We are not now that strength which in old days
Moved earth and heaven; that which we are, we are;
One equal temper of heroic hearts,
Made weak by time and fate, but strong in will
To strive, to seek, to find, and not to yield. 70

Morte d'Arthur

So all day long the noise of battle roll'd
Among the mountains by the winter sea;
Until King Arthur's table, man by man,
Had fallen in Lyonnesse about their Lord,
King Arthur: then, because his wound was deep,
The bold Sir Bedivere uplifted him,
Sir Bedivere, the last of all his knights,
And bore him to a chapel nigh the field,
A broken chancel with a broken cross,
That stood on a dark strait of barren land.   10
On one side lay the Ocean, and on one
Lay a great water, and the moon was full.
  Then spake King Arthur to Sir Bedivere:
'The sequel of to-day unsolders all
The goodliest fellowship of famous knights
Whereof this world holds record. Such a sleep
They sleep – the men I loved. I think that we
Shall never more, at any future time,
Delight our souls with talk of knightly deeds,
Walking about the gardens and the halls   20
Of Camelot, as in the days that were.
I perish by this people which I made, –
Tho' Merlin sware that I should come again
To rule once more – but let what will be, be,
I am so deeply smitten thro' the helm
That without help I cannot last till morn.
Thou therefore take my brand Excalibur,
Which was my pride: for thou rememberest how
In those old days, one summer noon, an arm
Rose up from out the bosom of the lake,   30
Clothed in white samite, mystic, wonderful,
Holding the sword – and how I row'd across
And took it, and have worn it, like a king:
And, wheresoever I am sung or told
In aftertime, this also shall be known:
But now delay not: take Excalibur,
And fling him far into the middle mere:

Watch what thou seëst, and lightly bring me word.'
  To him replied the bold Sir Bedivere:
'It is not meet, Sir King, to leave thee thus,   40
Aidless, alone, and smitten thro' the helm.
A little thing may harm a wounded man.
Yet I thy hest will all perform at full,
Watch what I see, and lightly bring thee word.'
  So saying, from the ruin'd shrine he stept
And in the moon athwart the place of tombs,
Where lay the mighty bones of ancient men,
Old knights, and over them the sea-wind sang
Shrill, chill, with flakes of foam. He, stepping down
By zig-zag paths, and juts of pointed rock,   50
Came on the shining levels of the lake.
  There drew he forth the brand Excalibur,
And o'er him, drawing it, the winter moon,
Brightening the skirts of a long cloud, ran forth
And sparkled keen with frost against the hilt:
For all the haft twinkled with diamond sparks,
Myriads of topaz-lights, and jacinth-work
Of subtlest jewellery. He gazed so long
That both his eyes were dazzled, as he stood,
This way and that dividing the swift mind,   60
In act to throw: but at the last it seem'd
Better to leave Excalibur conceal'd
There in the many-knotted waterflags,
That whistled stiff and dry about the marge.
So strode he back slow to the wounded King.
  Then spake King Arthur to Sir Bedivere:
'Hast thou perform'd my mission which I gave?
What is it thou hast seen? or what has heard?'
  And answer made the bold Sir Bedivere:
'I heard the ripple washing in the reeds,   70
And the wild water lapping on the crag.'
  To whom replied King Arthur, faint and pale:
'Thou hast betray'd thy nature and thy name,
Not rendering true answer, as beseem'd
Thy fëalty, nor like a noble knight:
For surer sign had follow'd, either hand,
Or voice, or else a motion of the mere.

This is a shameful thing for men to lie.
Yet now, I charge thee, quickly go again
As thou art lief and dear, and do the thing   80
I bad thee, watch, and lightly bring me word.'
    Then went Sir Bedivere the second time
Across the ridge, and paced beside the mere,
Counting the dewy pebbles, fix'd in thought;
But when he saw the wonder of the hilt,
How curiously and strangely chased, he smote
His palms together, and he cried aloud,
    'And if indeed I cast the brand away,
Surely a precious thing, one worthy note,
Should thus be lost for ever from the earth,   90
Which might have pleased the eyes of many men.
What good should follow this, if this were done?
What harm, undone? deep harm to disobey,
Seeing obedience is the bond of rule.
Were it well to obey then, if a king demand
An act unprofitable, against himself?
The King is sick, and knows not what he does.
What record, or what relic of my lord
Should be to aftertime, but empty breath
And rumours of a doubt? but were this kept,   100
Stored in some treasure-house of mighty kings,
Some one might show it at a joust of arms,
Saying, "King Arthur's sword, Excalibur,
Wrought by the lonely maiden of the Lake.
Nine years she wrought it, sitting in the deeps
Upon the hidden bases of the hills."
So might some old man speak in the aftertime
To all the people, winning reverence.
But now much honour and much fame were lost.'
    So spake he, clouded with his own conceit,   110
And hid Excalibur the second time,
And so strode back slow to the wounded King.
    Then spoke King Arthur, breathing heavily:
'What is it thou hast seen? or what hast heard?'
    And answer made the bold Sir Bedivere:
'I heard the water lapping on the crag,
And the long ripple washing in the reeds.'

To whom replied King Arthur, much in wrath:
'Ah, miserable and unkind, untrue,
Unknightly, traitor-hearted! Woe is me!   120
Authority forgets a dying king,
Laid widow'd of the power in his eye
That bow'd the will. I see thee what thou art,
For thou, the latest-left of all my knights,
In whom should meet the offices of all,
Thou wouldst betray me for the precious hilt;
Either from lust of gold, or like a girl
Valuing the giddy pleasure of the eyes.
Yet, for a man may fail in duty twice,
And the third time may prosper, get thee hence: 130
But, if thou spare to fling Excalibur,
I will arise and slay thee with my hands.'
   Then quickly rose Sir Bedivere, and ran,
And, leaping down the ridges lightly, plunged
Among the bulrush-beds, and clutch'd the sword,
And strongly wheel'd and threw it. The great brand
Made lightnings in the splendour of the moon,
And flashing round and round, and whirl'd in an arch,
Shot like a streamer of the northern morn,
Seen where the moving isles of winter shock   140
By night, with noises of the northern sea.
So flash'd and fell the brand Excalibur:
But ere he dipt the surface, rose an arm
Clothed in white samite, mystic, wonderful,
And caught him by the hilt, and brandish'd him
Three times, and drew him under in the mere.
And lightly went the other to the King.
   Then spoke King Arthur, drawing thicker breath:
'Now see I by thine eyes that this is done.
Speak out: what is it thou hast heard, or seen?'   150
   And answer made the bold Sir Bedivere:
'Sir King, I closed mine eyelids, lest the gems
Should blind my purpose, for I never saw,
Nor shall see, here or elsewhere, till I die,
Not tho' I live three lives of mortal men,
So great a miracle as yonder hilt.
Then with both hands I flung him, wheeling him;

But when I look'd again, behold an arm,
Clothed in white samite, mystic, wonderful,
That caught him by the hilt, and brandish'd him   160
Three times, and drew him under in the mere.'
     And answer made King Arthur, breathing hard:
'My end draws nigh; 'tis time that I were gone.
Make broad thy shoulders to receive my weight,
And bear me to the margin; yet I fear
My wound hath taken cold, and I shall die.'
     So saying, from the pavement he half rose,
Slowly, with pain, reclining on his arm,
And looking wistfully with wide blue eyes
As in a picture. Him Sir Bedivere   170
Remorsefully regarded thro' his tears,
And would have spoken, but he found not words,
Then took with care, and kneeling on one knee,
O'er both his shoulders drew the languid hands,
And rising bore him thro' the place of tombs.
     But, as he walk'd, King Arthur panted hard,
Like one that feels a nightmare on his bed
When all the house is mute. So sigh'd the King,
Muttering and murmuring at his ear, 'Quick, quick!
I fear it is too late, and I shall die.'   180
But the other swiftly strode from ridge to ridge,
Clothed with his breath, and looking, as he walk'd,
Larger than human on the frozen hills.
He heard the deep behind him, and a cry
Before. His own thought drove him, like a goad.
Dry clash'd his harness in the icy caves
And barren chasms, and all to left and right
The bare black cliff clang'd round him, as he based
His feet on juts of slippery crag that rang
Sharp-smitten with the dint of armed heels –   190
And on a sudden, lo! the level lake,
And the long glories of the winter moon.
     Then saw they how there hove a dusky barge,
Dark as a funeral scarf from stem to stern,
Beneath them; and descending they were ware
That all the decks were dense with stately forms
Black-stoled, black-hooded, like a dream – by these

Three Queens with crowns of gold – and from them rose
A cry that shiver'd to the tingling stars,
And, as it were one voice, an agony   200
Of lamentation, like a wind, that shrills
All night in a waste land, where no one comes,
Or hath come, since the making of the world.
    Then murmur'd Arthur, 'Place me in the barge,'
And to the barge they came. There those three Queens
Put forth their hands, and took the King, and wept.
But she, that rose the tallest of them all
And fairest, laid his head upon her lap,
And loosed the shatter'd casque, and chafed his hands,
And call'd him by his name, complaining loud,   210
And dropping bitter tears against his brow
Striped with dark blood: for all his face was white
And colourless, and like the wither'd moon
Smote by the fresh beam of the springing east;
And all his greaves and cuisses dash'd with drops
Of onset; and the light and lustrous curls –
That made his forehead like a rising sun
High from the daïs-throne – were parch'd with dust;
Or, clotted into points and hanging loose,
Mix'd with the knightly growth that fringed his lips.   220
So like a shatter'd column lay the King;
Not like that Arthur who, with lance in rest,
From spur to plume a star of tournament,
Shot thro' the lists at Camelot, and charged
Before the eyes of ladies and of kings.
    Then loudly cried the bold Sir Bedivere,
'Ah! my Lord Arthur, whither shall I go?
Where shall I hide my forehead and my eyes?
For now I see the true old times are dead,
When every morning brought a noble chance,   230
And every chance brought out a noble knight.
Such times have been not since the light that led
The holy Elders with the gift of myrrh.
But now the whole ROUND TABLE is dissolved
Which was an image of the mighty world;
And I, the last, go forth companionless,
And the days darken round me, and the years,

Among new men, strange faces, other minds.'
 And slowly answered Arthur from the barge:
'The old order changeth, yielding place to new,   240
And God fulfils Himself in many ways,
Lest one good custom should corrupt the world.
Comfort thyself: what comfort is in me?
I have lived my life, and that which I have done
May He within Himself make pure! but thou,
If thou shouldst never see my face again,
Pray for my soul. More things are wrought by prayer
Than this world dreams of. Wherefore, let thy voice
Rise like a fountain for me night and day.
For what are men better than sheep or goats   250
That nourish a blind life within the brain,
If, knowing God, they lift not hands of prayer
Both for themselves and those who call them friend?
For so the whole round earth is every way
Bound by gold chains about the feet of God.
But now farewell. I am going a long way
With these thou seëst – if indeed I go –
(For all my mind is clouded with a doubt)
To the island-valley of Avilion;
Where falls not hail, or rain, or any snow,   260
Nor ever wind blows loudly; but it lies
Deep-meadow'd, happy, fair with orchard-lawns
And bowery hollows crown'd with summer sea,
Where I will heal me of my grievous wound.'
 So said he, and the barge with oar and sail
Moved from the brink, like some full-breasted swan
That, fluting a wild carol ere her death,
Ruffles her pure cold plume, and takes the flood
With swarthy webs. Long stood Sir Bedivere
Revolving many memories, till the hull   270
Look'd one black dot against the verge of dawn,
And on the mere the wailing died away.

'Break, Break, Break . . .'

Break, break, break,
On thy cold gray stones, O Sea!
And I would that my tongue could utter
The thoughts that arise in me.

O well for the fisherman's boy,
That he shouts with his sister at play!
O well for the sailor lad,
That he sings in his boat on the bay!

And the stately ships go on
To their haven under the hill;   10
But O for the touch of a vanish'd hand,
And the sound of a voice that is still!

Break, break, break,
At the foot of thy crags, O Sea!
But the tender grace of a day that is dead
Will never come back to me.

Locksley Hall

Comrades, leave me here a little, while as yet 'tis early
    morn:
Leave me here, and when you want me, sound upon the
    bugle-horn.

'Tis the place, and all around it, as of old, the curlews call,
Dreary gleams about the moorland flying over Locksley
    Hall;

Locksley Hall, that in the distance overlooks the sandy
    tracts,
And the hollow ocean-ridges roaring into cataracts.

Many a night from yonder ivied casement, ere I went to
    rest,
Did I look on great Orion sloping slowly to the West.

Many a night I saw the Pleiads, rising thro' the mellow
    shade,
Glitter like a swarm of fire-flies tangled in a silver braid.   10

Here about the beach I wander'd, nourishing a youth
    sublime
With the fairy tales of science, and the long result of Time;

When the centuries behind me like a fruitful land reposed;
When I clung to all the present for the promise that it
    closed:

When I dipt into the future far as human eye could see;
Saw the Vision of the world, and all the wonder that would
    be. —

In the Spring a fuller crimson comes upon the robin's
    breast;
In the Spring the wanton lapwing gets himself another
    crest;

In the Spring a livelier iris changes on the burnish'd dove;
In the Spring a young man's fancy lightly turns to thoughts
    of love.   20

Then her cheek was pale and thinner than should be for
    one so young,
And her eyes on all my motions with a mute observance
    hung.

And I said, 'My cousin Amy, speak, and speak the truth to
    me,
Trust me, cousin, all the current of my being sets to thee.'

On her pallid cheek and forehead came a colour and a light,
As I have seen the rosy red flushing in the northern night.

And she turn'd – her bosom shaken with a sudden storm of
   sighs –
All the spirit deeply dawning in the dark of hazel eyes –

Saying, 'I have hid my feelings, fearing they should do me
   wrong;'
Saying, 'Dost thou love me, cousin?' weeping, 'I have loved
   thee long.'   30

Love took up the glass of Time, and turn'd it in his glowing
   hands;
Every moment, lightly shaken, ran itself in golden sands.

Love took up the harp of Life, and smote on all the chords
   with might;
Smote the chord of Self, that, trembling, pass'd in music out
   of sight.

Many a morning on the moorland did we hear the copses
   ring,
And her whisper throng'd my pulses with the fullness of the
   Spring.

Many an evening by the waters did we watch the stately
   ships,
And our spirits rush'd together at the touching of the lips.

O my cousin, shallow-hearted! O my Amy, mine no more!
O the dreary, dreary moorland! O the barren, barren shore!   40

Falser than all fancy fathoms, falser than all songs have
   sung,
Puppet to a father's threat, and servile to a shrewish
   tongue!

Is it well to wish thee happy?—having known me—to
   decline
On a range of lower feelings and a narrower heart than
   mine!

Yet it shall be: thou shall lower to his level day by day,
What is fine within thee growing coarse to sympathise with
    clay.

As the husband is, the wife is: thou art mated with a clown,
And the grossness of his nature will have weight to drag
    thee down.

He will hold thee, when his passion shall have spent its
    novel force,
Something better than his dog, a little dearer than his
    horse.   50

What is this? his eyes are heavy: think not they are glazed
    with wine.
Go to him: it is thy duty: kiss him: take his hand in thine.

It may be my lord is weary, that his brain is overwrought:
Soothe him with thy finer fancies, touch him with thy
    lighter thought.

He will answer to the purpose, easy things to understand –
Better thou wert dead before me, tho' I slew thee with my
    hand!

Better thou and I were lying, hidden from the heart's
    disgrace,
Roll'd in one another's arms, and silent in a last embrace.

Cursed be the social wants that sin against the strength of
    youth!
Cursed be the social lies that warp us from the living truth!   60

Cursed be the sickly forms that err from honest Nature's
    rule!
Cursed be the gold that gilds the straiten'd forehead of the
    fool!

Well – 'tis well that I should bluster! – Hadst thou less
    unworthy proved –

Would to God – for I had loved thee more than ever wife
   was loved.

Am I mad, that I should cherish that which bears but bitter
   fruit?
I will pluck it from my bosom, tho' my heart be at the root.

Never, tho' my mortal summers to such length of years
   should come
As the many-winter'd crow that leads the clanging rookery
   home.

Where is comfort? in division of the records of the mind?
Can I part her from herself, and love her, as I knew her,
   kind?   70

I remember one that perish'd: sweetly did she speak and
   move:
Such a one do I remember, whom to look at was to love.

Can I think of her as dead, and love her for the love she
   bore?
No – she never loved me truly: love is love for evermore.

Comfort? comfort scorn'd of devils! this is truth the poet
   sings,
That a sorrow's crown of sorrow is remembering happier
   things.

Drug thy memories, lest thou learn it, lest thy heart be put
   to proof,
In the dead unhappy night, and when the rain is on the
   roof.

Like a dog, he hunts in dreams, and thou art staring at the
   wall,
Where the dying night-lamp flickers, and the shadows rise
   and fall.   80

Then a hand shall pass before thee, pointing to his drunken
   sleep,

To thy widow'd marriage-pillows, to the tears that thou
    wilt weep.

Thou shalt hear the 'Never, never,' whisper'd by the
    phantom years,
And a song from out the distance in the ringing of thine
    ears;

And an eye shall vex thee, looking ancient kindness on thy
    pain.
Turn thee, turn thee on thy pillow: get thee to thy rest
    again.

Nay, but Nature brings thee solace; for a tender voice will
    cry.
'Tis a purer life than thine; a lip to drain thy trouble dry.

Baby lips will laugh me down: my latest rival brings thee
    rest.
Baby fingers, waxen touches, press me from the mother's
    breast.   90

O, the child too clothes the father with a dearness not his
    due.
Half is thine and half is his: it will be worthy of the two.

O, I see thee old and formal, fitted to thy petty part,
With a little hoard of maxims preaching down a daughter's
    heart.

'They were dangerous guides the feelings – she herself was
    not exempt –
Truly, she herself had suffer'd' – Perish in thy self-
    contempt!

Overlive it – lower yet – be happy! wherefore should I care?
I myself must mix with action, lest I wither by despair.

What is that which I should turn to, lighting upon days like
    these?

Every door is barr'd with gold, and opens but to golden
    keys.   100

Every gate is throng'd with suitors, all the markets
    overflow.
I have but an angry fancy: what is that which I should do?

I had been content to perish, falling on the foeman's
    ground,
When the ranks are roll'd in vapour, and the winds are laid
    with sound.

But the jingling of the guinea helps the hurt that Honour
    feels,
And the nations do but murmur, snarling at each other's
    heels.

Can I but relive in sadness? I will turn that earlier page.
Hide me from my deep emotion, O thou wondrous Mother-
    Age!

Make me feel the wild pulsation that I felt before the strife,
When I heard my days before me, and the tumult of my life;   110

Yearning for the large excitement that the coming years
    would yield,
Eager-hearted as a boy when first he leaves his father's
    field,

And at night along the dusky highway near and nearer
    drawn,
Sees in heaven the light of London flaring like a dreary
    dawn;

And his spirit leaps within him to be gone before him then,
Underneath the light he looks at, in among the throngs of
    men:

Men, my brothers, men the workers, ever reaping
    something new:

That which they have done but earnest of the things that
    they shall do:

For I dipt into the future, far as human eye could see,
Saw the Vision of the world, and all the wonder that would
    be;   120

Saw the heavens fill with commerce, argosies of magic sails,
Pilots of the purple twilight, dropping down with costly
    bales;

Heard the heavens fill with shouting, and there rain'd a
    ghastly dew
From the nations' airy navies grappling in the central blue;

Far along the world-wide whisper of the south-wind
    rushing warm,
With the standards of the peoples plunging thro' the
    thunder-storm;

Till the war-drum throbb'd no longer, and the battle-flags
    were furl'd
In the Parliament of man, the Federation of the world.

There the common sense of most shall hold a fretful realm
    in awe,
And the kindly earth shall slumber, lapt in universal law.   130

So I triumph'd ere my passion sweeping thro' me left me
    dry,
Left me with the palsied heart, and left me with the
    jaundiced eye;

Eye, to which all order festers, all things here are out of
    joint:
Science moves, but slowly slowly, creeping on from point to
    point:

Slowly comes a hungry people, as a lion creeping nigher,

Glares at one that nods and winks behind a slowly-dying
     fire.

Yes I doubt not thro' the ages one increasing purpose runs,
And the thoughts of men are widen'd with the process of
     the suns.

What is that to him that reaps not harvest of his youthful
     joys,
Tho' the deep heart of existence beat for ever like a boy's?   140

Knowledge comes, but wisdom lingers, and I linger on the
     shore,
And the individual withers, and the world is more and
     more.

Knowledge comes, but wisdom lingers, and he bears a
     laden breast,
Full of sad experience, moving toward the stillness of his
     rest.

Hark, my merry comrades call me, sounding on the bugle-
     horn,
They to whom my foolish passion were a target for their
     scorn:

Shall it not be scorn to me to harp on such a moulder'd
     string?
I am shamed thro' all my nature to have loved so slight a
     thing.

Weakness to be wroth with weakness! woman's pleasure,
     woman's pain –
Nature made them blinder motions bounded in a shallower
     brain: 150

Woman is the lesser man, and all thy passions, match'd
     with mine,
Are as moonlight unto sunlight, and as water unto wine –

Here at least, where nature sickens, nothing. Ah, for some
    retreat
Deep in younger shining Orient, where my life began to
    beat;

Where in wild Mahratta-battle fell my father evil-starr'd; –
I was left a trampled orphan, and a selfish uncle's ward.

Or to burst all links of habit – there to wander far away,
On from island unto island at the gateways of the day.

Larger constellations burning, mellow moons and happy
    skies,
Breadths of tropic shade and palms in cluster, knots of
    Paradise.   160

Never comes the trader, never floats an European flag,
Slides the bird o'er lustrous woodland, swings the trailer
    from the crag;

Droops the heavy-blossom'd bower, hangs the heavy-
    fruited tree –
Summer isles of Eden lying in dark-purple spheres of sea.

There methinks would be enjoyment more than in this
    march of mind,
In the steamship, in the railway, in the thoughts that shake
    mankind.

There the passions cramp'd no longer shall have scope and
    breathing space;
I will take some savage woman, she shall rear my dusky
    race.

Iron jointed, supple-sinew'd, they shall dive, and they shall
    run,
Catch the wild goat by the hair, and hurl their lances in the
    sun;   170

Whistle back the parrot's call, and leap the rainbows of the
    brooks,

Not with blinded eyesight poring over miserable books –

Fool, again the dream, the fancy! but I *know* my words are wild,
But I count the gray barbarian lower than the Christian child.

I, to herd with narrow foreheads, vacant of our glorious gains,
Like a beast with lower pleasures, like a beast with lower pains!

Mated with a squalid savage – what to me were sun or clime?
I the heir of all the ages, in the foremost files of time –

I that rather held it better men should perish one by one,
Than that earth should stand at gaze like Joshua's moon in Ajalon!   180

Not in vain the distance beacons. Forward, forward let us range,
Let the great world spin for ever down the ringing grooves of change.

Thro' the shadow of the globe we sweep into the younger day:
Better fifty years of Europe than a cycle of Cathay.

Mother-Age (for mine I knew not) help me as when life begun:
Rift the hills, and roll the waters, flash the lightnings, weigh the Sun.

O, I see the crescent promise of my spirit hath not set.
Ancient founts of inspiration well thro' all my fancy yet.

Howsoever these things be, a long farewell to Locksley Hall!

Now for me the woods may wither, now for me the roof-
   tree fall.   190

Comes a vapour from the margin, blackening over heath
   and holt,
Cramming all the blast before it, in its breast a thunderbolt.

Let it fall on Locksley Hall, with rain or hail, or fire or snow;
For the mighty wind arises, roaring seaward, and I go.

The Golden Year

Well, you shall have that song which Leonard wrote:
It was last summer on a tour in Wales:
Old James was with me: we that day had been
Up Snowdon; and I wish'd for Leonard there,
And found him in Llanberis: then we crost
Between the lakes, and clamber'd half way up
The counter side; and that same song of his
He told me; for I banter'd him, and swore
They said he lived shut up within himself,
A tongue-tied Poet in the feverous days,   10
That, setting the *how much* before the *how*,
Cry, like the daughters of the horseleech, 'Give,
Cram us with all,' but count not me the herd!

   To which 'They call me what they will,' he said:
'But I was born too late: the fair new forms,
That float about the threshold of an age,
Like truths of Science waiting to be caught –
Catch me who can, and make the catcher crown'd –
Are taken by the forelock. Let it be.
But if you care indeed to listen, hear   20
These measured words, my work of yestermorn.

   'We sleep and wake and sleep, but all things move;
The Sun flies forward to his brother Sun;

The dark Earth follows wheeled in her ellipse;
And human things returning on themselves
Move onward, leading up the golden year.
  'Ah tho' the times, when some new thought can bud,
Are but as poets' seasons when they flower,
Yet oceans daily gaining on the land,
Have ebb and flow conditioning their march,   30
And slow and sure comes up the golden year.
  'When wealth no more shall rest in mounded heaps,
But smit with freër light shall slowly melt
In many streams to fatten lower lands,
And light shall spread, and man be liker man
Thro' all the season of the golden year.
  'Shall eagles not be eagles? wrens be wrens?
If all the world were falcons, what of that?
The wonder of the eagle were the less,
But he not less the eagle. Happy days   40
Roll onward, leading up the golden year.
  'Fly, happy happy sails, and bear the Press;
Fly happy with the mission of the Cross;
Knit land to land, and blowing havenward
With silks, and fruits, and spices, clear of toll,
Enrich the markets of the golden year.
  'But we grow old. Ah! when shall all men's good
Be each man's rule, and universal Peace
Lie like a shaft of light across the land,
And like a lane of beams athwart the sea,   50
Thro' all the circle of the golden year?'

  Thus far he flow'd, and ended; whereupon
'Ah, folly!' in mimic cadence answered James –
'Ah, folly! for it lies so far away,
Not in our time, nor in our children's time,
'Tis like the second world to us that live;
'Twere all as one to fix our hopes on Heaven
As on this vision of the golden year.'

  With that he struck his staff against the rocks
And broke it, – James, – you know him, – old, but full   60

Of force and choler, and firm upon his feet,
And like an oaken stock in winter woods,
O'erflourish'd with the hoary clematis:
Then added, all in heat:
      'What stuff is this!
Old writers push'd the happy season back, –
The more fools they, – we forward: dreamers both:
You most, that in an age, when every hour
Must sweat her sixty minutes to the death,
Live on, God love us, as if the seedsman, rapt
Upon the teeming harvest, should not plunge   70
His hand into the bag: but well I know
That unto him who works, and feels he works,
This same grand year is ever at the doors.'

He spoke; and, high above, I heard them blast
The steep slate-quarry, and the great echo flap
And buffet round the hills, from bluff to bluff.

from The Princess
'The Splendour Falls . . .'

The splendour falls on castle walls
  And snowy summits old in story:
The long light shakes across the lakes,
  And the wild cataract leaps in glory.
Blow, bugle, blow, set the wild echoes flying,
Blow, bugle; answer, echoes, dying, dying, dying.
  O hark, O hear! how thin and clear,
   And thinner, clearer, farther going!
  O sweet and far from cliff and scar
   The horns of Elfland faintly blowing!   10
Blow, let us hear the purple glens replying:

Blow, bugle; answers, echoes, dying, dying, dying.
  O love, they die in yon rich sky,
    They faint on hill or field or river:
  Our echoes roll from soul to soul,
    And grow for ever and for ever.
Blow, bugle, blow, set the wild echoes flying,
And answer, echoes, answer, dying, dying, dying.

'Tears, Idle Tears . . .'

Tears, idle tears, I know not what they mean,
Tears from the depth of some divine despair
Rise in the heart, and gather to the eyes,
In looking on the happy Autumn-fields,
And thinking of the days that are no more.

Fresh as the first beam glittering on a sail,
That brings our friends up from the underworld,
Sad as the last which reddens over one
That sinks with all we love below the verge;
So sad, so fresh, the days that are no more.   10

Ah, sad and strange as in dark summer dawns
The earliest pipe of half-awaken'd birds
To dying ears, when unto dying eyes
The casement slowly grows a glimmering square;
So sad, so strange, the days that are no more.

Dear as remember'd kisses after death,
And sweet as those by hopeless fancy feign'd
On lips that are for others; deep as love,
Deep as first love, and wild with all regret;
O Death in Life, the days that are no more.   20

'Now Sleeps the Crimson Petal . . .'

Now sleeps the crimson petal, now the white;
Nor waves the cypress in the palace walk;
Nor winks the gold fin in the porphyry font:
The fire-fly wakens: waken thou with me.

Now droops the milkwhite peacock like a ghost,
And like a ghost she glimmers on to me.

Now lies the Earth all Danaë to the stars,
And all thy heart lies open unto me.

Now slides the silent meteor on, and leaves
A shining furrow, as thy thoughts in me.   10

Now folds the lily all her sweetness up,
And slips into the bosom of the lake:
So fold thyself, my dearest, thou, and slip
Into my bosom and be lost in me.

'Come Down, O Maid . . .'

Come down, O maid, from yonder mountain height:
What pleasure lives in height (the shepherd sang)
In height and cold, the splendour of the hills?
But cease to move so near the Heavens, and cease
To glide a sunbeam by the blasted Pine,
To sit a star upon the sparkling spire;
And come, for Love is of the valley, come,
For Love is of the valley, come thou down
And find him; by the happy threshold, he,
Or hand in hand with Plenty in the maize,   10
Or red with spirted purple of the vats,
Or foxlike in the vine; nor cares to walk

With Death and Morning on the silver horns,
Nor wilt thou snare him in the white ravine,
Nor find him dropt upon the firths of ice,
That huddling slant in furrow-cloven falls
To roll the torrent out of dusky doors:
But follow; let the torrent dance thee down
To find him in the valley; let the wild
Lean-headed Eagles yelp alone, and leave   20
The monstrous ledges there to slope, and spill
Their thousand wreaths of dangling water-smoke,
That like a broken purpose waste in air:
So waste not thou; but come; for all the vales
Await thee; azure pillars of the hearth
Arise to thee; the children call, and I
Thy shepherd pipe, and sweet is every sound,
Sweeter thy voice, but every sound is sweet;
Myriads of rivulets hurrying thro' the lawn,
The moan of doves in immemorial elms,   30
And murmuring of innumerable bees.

from In Memoriam A. H. H.

OBIT MDCCCXXXIII

1

I held it truth, with him who sings
    To one clear harp in divers tones,
    That men may rise on stepping-stones
Of their dead selves to higher things.

But who shall so forecast the years
    And find in loss a gain to match?
    Or reach a hand thro' time to catch
The far-off interest of tears?

Let Love clasp Grief lest both be drown'd,
    Let darkness keep her raven gloss: 10
    Ah, sweeter to be drunk with loss,
To dance with death, to beat the ground,

Than that the victor Hours should scorn
    The long result of love, and boast,
    'Behold the man that loved and lost,
But all he was is overworn.'

2

Old Yew, which graspest at the stones
    That name the under-lying dead,
    Thy fibres net the dreamless head,
Thy roots are wrapt about the bones.

The seasons bring the flower again,
    And bring the firstling to the flock;
    And in the dusk of thee, the clock
Beats out the little lives of men.

O not for thee the glow, the bloom,
    Who changest not in any gale,   10
    Nor branding summer suns avail
To touch thy thousand years of gloom:

And gazing on thee, sullen tree,
    Sick for thy stubborn hardihood,
    I seem to fail from out my blood
And grow incorporate into thee.

3

O Sorrow, cruel fellowship,
    O Priestess in the vaults of Death,
    O sweet and bitter in a breath,
What whispers from thy lying lip?

'The stars,' she whispers, 'blindly run;
    A web is wov'n across the sky;

From out waste places comes a cry,
And murmurs from the dying sun:

'And all the phantom, Nature, stands –
    With all the music in her tone,   10
    A hollow echo of my own, –
A hollow form with empty hands.'

And shall I take a thing so blind,
    Embrace her as my natural good;
    Or crush her, like a vice of blood,
Upon the threshold of the mind?

5

I sometimes hold it half a sin
    To put in words the grief I feel;
    For words, like Nature, half reveal
And half conceal the Soul within.

But, for the unquiet heart and brain,
    A use in measured language lies;
    The sad mechanic exercise,
Like dull narcotics, numbing pain.

In words, like weeds, I'll wrap me o'er,
    Like coarsest clothes against the cold: 10
    But that large grief which these enfold
Is given in outline and no more.

6

One writes, that 'Other friends remain,'
    That 'Loss is common to the race' –
    And common is the commonplace,
And vacant chaff well meant for grain.

That loss is common would not make
    My own less bitter, rather more:

Too common! Never morning wore
To evening, but some heart did break.

O father, whereso'er thou be,
    Who pledgest now thy gallant son;   10
    A shot, ere half thy draught be done,
Hath still'd the life that beat from thee.

O mother, praying God will save
    Thy sailor, – while thy head is bow'd,
    His heavy-shotted hammock-shroud
Drops in his vast and wandering grave.

Ye know no more than I who wrought
    At that last hour to please him well;
    Who mused on all I had to tell,
And something written, something thought;   20

Expecting still his advent home;
    And ever met him on his way
    With wishes, thinking, 'here to-day,'
Or 'here to-morrow will he come.'

O somewhere, meek, unconscious dove,
    That sittest ranging golden hair;
    And glad to find thyself so fair,
Poor child, that waitest for thy love!

For now her father's chimney glows
    In expectation of a guest;   30
    And thinking 'this will please him best,'
She takes a riband or a rose;

For he will see them on to-night;
    And with the thought her colour burns;
    And, having left the glass, she turns
Once more to set a ringlet right;

And, even when she turn'd, the curse
    Had fallen, and her future Lord

Was drown'd in passing thro' the ford,
Or kill'd in falling from his horse.   40

O what to her shall be the end?
     And what to me remains of good?
     To her, perpetual maidenhood,
And unto me no second friend.

7

Dark house, by which once more I stand
     Here in the long unlovely street,
     Doors, where my heart was used to beat
So quickly, waiting for a hand,

A hand that can be clasp'd no more —
     Behold me, for I cannot sleep,
     And like a guilty thing I creep
At earliest morning to the door.

He is not here: but far away
     The noise of life begins again,   10
     And ghastly thro' the drizzling rain
On the bald street breaks the blank day.

21

I sing to him that rests below,
     And, since the grasses round me wave,
     I take the grasses of the grave,
And make them pipes whereon to blow.

The traveller hears me now and then,
     And sometimes harshly will he speak:
     'This fellow would make weakness weak,
And melt the waxen hearts of men.'

Another answers, 'Let him be,
     He loves to make parade of pain,   10

That with his piping he may gain
The praise that comes to constancy.'

A third is wroth: 'Is this an hour
 For private sorrow's barren song,
 When more and more the people throng
The chairs and thrones of civil power?

'A time to sicken and to swoon,
 When Science reaches forth her arms
 To feel from world to world, and charms
Her secret from the latest moon?'   20

Behold, ye speak an idle thing:
 Ye never knew the sacred dust:
 I do but sing because I must,
And pipe but as the linnets sing:

And one is glad; her note is gay,
 For now her little ones have ranged;
 And one is sad; her note is changed,
Because her brood is stol'n away.

27

I envy not in any moods
 The captive void of noble rage,
 The linnet born within the cage,
That never knew the summer woods:

I envy not the beast that takes
 His license in the field of time,
 Unfetter'd by the sense of crime,
To whom a conscience never wakes;

Nor, what may count itself as blest,
 The heart that never plighted troth   10
 But stagnates in the weeds of sloth;
Nor any want-begotten rest.

I hold it true, whate'er befall;
     I feel it, when I sorrow most;
     'Tis better to have loved and lost
Than never to have loved at all.

39

Old warder of these buried bones,
     And answering now my random stroke
     With fruitful cloud and living smoke,
Dark yew, that graspest at the stones

And dippest toward the dreamless head,
     To thee too comes the golden hour
     When flower is feeling after flower;
But Sorrow – fixt upon the dead,

And darkening the dark graves of men, –
     What whisper'd from her lying lips?   10
     Thy gloom is kindled at the tips,
And passes into gloom again.

50

Be near me when my light is low,
     When the blood creeps, and the nerves prick
     And tingle; and the heart is sick,
And all the wheels of Being slow.

Be near me when the sensuous frame
     Is rack'd with pangs that conquer trust;
     And Time, a maniac scattering dust,
And Life, a Fury slinging flame.

Be near me when my faith is dry,
     And men the flies of latter spring,   10
     That lay their eggs, and sting and sing
And weave their petty cells and die.

Be near me when I fade away,
    To point the term of human strife,
    And on the low dark verge of life
The twilight of eternal day.

51

Do we indeed desire the dead
    Should still be near us at our side?
    Is there no baseness we would hide?
No inner vileness that we dread?

Shall he for whose applause I strove,
    I had such reverence for his blame,
    See with clear eye some hidden shame
And I be lessen'd in his love?

I wrong the grave with fears untrue:
    Shall love be blamed for want of faith?   10
    There must be wisdom with great Death:
The dead shall look me thro' and thro'.

Be near us when we climb or fall:
    Ye watch, like God, the rolling hours
    With larger other eyes than ours,
To make allowance for us all.

54

Oh yet we trust that somehow good
    Will be the final goal of ill,
    To pangs of nature, sins of will,
Defects of doubt, and taints of blood;

That nothing walks with aimless feet;
    That not one life shall be destroy'd,
    Or cast as rubbish to the void,
When God hath made the pile complete;

That not a worm is cloven in vain;
    That not a moth with vain desire   10

Is shrivell'd in a fruitless fire,
Or but subserves another's gain.

Behold, we know not anything;
    I can but trust that good shall fall
    At last – far off – at last, to all,
And every winter change to spring.

So runs my dream: but what am I?
    An infant crying in the night:
    An infant crying for the light:
And with no language but a cry.   20

55

The wish, that of the living whole
    No life may fail beyond the grave,
    Derives it not from what we have
The likest God within the soul?

Are God and Nature then at strife,
    That Nature lends such evil dreams?
    So careful of the type she seems,
So careless of the single life;

That I, considering everywhere
    Her secret meaning in her deeds,   10
    And finding that of fifty seeds
She often brings but one to bear,

I falter where I firmly trod,
    And falling with my weight of cares
    Upon the great world's altar-stairs
That slope thro' darkness up to God,

I stretch lame hands of faith, and grope,
    And gather dust and chaff, and call

To what I feel is Lord of all,
And faintly trust the larger hope.   20

56

'So careful of the type?' but no.
   From scarped cliff and quarried stone
   She cries, 'A thousand types are gone:
I care for nothing, all shall go.

'Thou makest thine appeal to me:
   I bring to life, I bring to death:
   The spirit does but mean the breath:
I know no more.' And he, shall he,

Man, her last work, who seem'd so fair,
   Such splendid purpose in his eyes,   10
   Who roll'd the psalm to wintry skies,
Who built him fanes of fruitless prayer,

Who trusted God was love indeed
   And love Creation's final law –
   Tho' Nature, red in tooth and claw
With ravine, shriek'd against his creed –

Who loved, who suffer'd countless ills,
   Who battled for the True, the Just,
   Be blown about the desert dust,
Or seal'd within the iron hills?   20

No more? A monster then, a dream,
   A discord. Dragons of the prime,
   That tare each other in their slime,
Were mellow music match'd with him.

O life as futile, then, as frail!
   O for thy voice to soothe and bless!
   What hope of answer, or redress?
Behind the veil, behind the veil.

64

Dost thou look back on what hath been,
    As some divinely gifted man,
    Whose life in low estate began
And on a simple village green;

Who breaks his birth's invidious bar,
    And grasps the skirts of happy chance,
    And breasts the blows of circumstance,
And grapples with his evil star;

Who makes by force his merit known
    And lives to clutch the golden keys,   10
    To mould a mighty state's decrees,
And shape the whisper of the throne;

And moving up from high to higher,
    Becomes on Fortune's crowning slope
    The pillar of a people's hope,
The centre of a world's desire;

Yet feels, as in a pensive dream,
    When all his active powers are still,
    A distant dearness in the hill,
A secret sweetness in the stream,   20

The limit of his narrower fate,
    While yet beside its vocal springs
    He play'd at counsellors and kings,
With one that was his earliest mate;

Who ploughs with pain his native lea
    And reaps the labour of his hands,
    Or in the furrow musing stands;
'Does my old friend remember me?'

70

I cannot see the features right,
    When on the gloom I strive to paint
    The face I know; the hues are faint
And mix with hollow masks of night;

Cloud-towers by ghostly masons wrought,
    A gulf that ever shuts and gapes,
    A hand that points, and palled shapes
In shadowy thoroughfares of thought;

And crowds that stream from yawning doors,
    And shoals of pucker'd faces drive;   10
    Dark bulks that tumble half alive,
And lazy lengths on boundless shores;

Till all at once beyond the will
    I hear a wizard music roll,
    And thro' a lattice on the soul
Looks thy fair face and makes it still.

74

As sometimes in a dead man's face,
    To those that watch it more and more,
    A likeness, hardly seen before,
Comes out – to some one of his race:

So, dearest, now thy brows are cold,
    I see thee what thou art, and know
    Thy likeness to the wise below,
Thy kindred with the great of old.

But there is more than I can see,
    And what I see I leave unsaid,   10
    Nor speak it, knowing Death has made
His darkness beautiful with thee.

77

What hope is here for modern rhyme
    To him, who turns a musing eye
    On songs, and deeds, and lives, that lie
Foreshorten'd in the tract of time?

These mortal lullabies of pain
    May bind a book, may line a box,
    May serve to curl a maiden's locks,
Or when a thousand moons shall wane

A man upon a stall may find,
    And, passing, turn the page that tells   10
    A grief, then changed to something else,
Sung by a long-forgotten mind.

But what of that? My darken'd ways
    Shall ring with music all the same;
    To breathe my loss is more than fame,
To utter love more sweet than praise.

90

He tasted love with half his mind,
    Nor ever drank the inviolate spring
    Where nighest heaven, who first could fling
This bitter seed among mankind;

That could the dead, whose dying eyes
    Were closed with wail, resume their life,
    They would but find in child and wife
An iron welcome when they rise;

'Twas well, indeed, when warm with wine,
    To pledge them with a kindly tear,   10
    To talk them o'er, to wish them here,
To count their memories half divine;

But if they came who past away,
    Behold their brides in other hands;
    The hard heir strides about their lands,
And will not yield them for a day.

Yea, tho' their sons were none of these,
    Not less the yet-loved sire would make

Confusion worse than death, and shake
The pillars of domestic peace.　　　20

Ah dear, but come thou back to me:
　　Whatever change the years have wrought,
　　I find not yet one lonely thought
That cries against my wish for thee.

93

I shall not see thee. Dare I say
　　No spirit ever brake the band
　　That stays him from the native land
Where first he walk'd when claspt in clay?

No visual shade of some one lost,
　　But he, the Spirit himself, may come
　　Where all the nerve of sense is numb;
Spirit to Spirit, Ghost to Ghost.

O, therefore from thy sightless range
　　With gods in unconjectured bliss,　　　10
　　O, from the distance of the abyss
Of tenfold-complicated change,

Descend, and touch, and enter; hear
　　The wish too strong for words to name;
　　That in this blindness of the frame
My Ghost may feel that thine is near.

96

You say, but with no touch of scorn,
　　Sweet-hearted, you whose light-blue eyes
　　Are tender over drowning flies,
You tell me, doubt is Devil-born.

I know not: one indeed I knew
　　In many a subtle question versed,

Who touch'd a jarring lyre at first,
But ever strove to make it true:

Perplext in faith, but pure in deeds,
    At last he beat his music out.   10
    There lives more faith in honest doubt,
Believe me, than in half the creeds.

He fought his doubts and gather'd strength,
    He would not make his judgment blind,
    He faced the spectres of the mind
And laid them: thus he came at length

To find a stronger faith his own;
    And Power was with him in the night,
    Which makes the darkness and the light,
And dwells not in the light alone,   20

But in the darkness and the cloud,
    As over Sinaï's peaks of old,
    While Israel made their gods of gold,
Altho' the trumpet blew so loud.

100

I climb the hill: from end to end
    Of all the landscape underneath,
    I find no place that does not breathe
Some gracious memory of my friend;

No gray old grange, or lonely fold,
    Or low morass and whispering reed,
    Or simple stile from mead to mead,
Or sheepwalk up the windy wold;

Nor hoary knoll of ash and haw
    That hears the latest linnet trill,   10
    Nor quarry trench'd along the hill
And haunted by the wrangling daw;

Nor runlet tinkling from the rock;
  Nor pastoral rivulet that swerves
  To left and right thro' meadowy curves,
That feed the mothers of the flock;

But each has pleased a kindred eye,
  And each reflects a kindlier day;
  And, leaving these, to pass away,
I think once more he seems to die.   20

101

Unwatch'd, the garden bough shall sway,
  The tender blossom flutter down,
  Unloved, that beech will gather brown,
This maple burn itself away;

Unloved, the sun-flower, shining fair,
  Ray round with flames her disk of seed,
  And many a rose-carnation feed
With summer spice the humming air;

Unloved, by many a sandy bar,
  The brook shall babble down the plain, 10
  At noon or when the lesser wain
Is twisting round the polar star;

Uncared for, gird the windy grove,
  And flood the haunts of hern and crake;
  Or into silver arrows break
The sailing moon in creek and cove;

Till from the garden and the wild
  A fresh association blow,
  And year by year the landscape grow
Familiar to the stranger's child;   20

As year by year the labourer tills
  His wonted glebe, or lops the glades;

And year by year our memory fades
From all the circle of the hills.

105

To-night ungather'd let us leave
    This laurel, let this holly stand:
    We live within the stranger's land,
And strangely falls our Christmas-eve.

Our father's dust is left alone
    And silent under other snows:
    There in due time the woodbine blows,
The violet comes, but we are gone.

No more shall wayward grief abuse
    The genial hour with mask and mime;   10
    For change of place, like growth of time,
Has broke the bond of dying use.

Let cares that petty shadows cast,
    By which our lives are chiefly proved,
    A little spare the night I loved,
And hold it solemn to the past.

But let no footstep beat the floor,
    Nor bowl of wassail mantle warm:
    For who would keep an ancient form
Thro' which the spirit breathes no more?   20

Be neither song, nor game, nor feast;
    Nor harp be touch'd, nor flute be blown;
    No dance, no motion, save alone
What lightens in the lucid east

Of rising worlds by yonder wood.
    Long sleeps the summer in the seed;
    Run out your measured arcs, and lead
The closing cycle rich in good.

106

Ring out, wild bells, to the wild sky,
    The flying cloud, the frosty light:
    The year is dying in the night;
Ring out, wild bells, and let him die.

Ring out the old, ring in the new,
    Ring, happy bells, across the snow:
    The year is going, let him go;
Ring out the false, ring in the true.

Ring out the grief that saps the mind,
    For those that here we see no more;   10
    Ring out the feud of rich and poor,
Ring in redress to all mankind.

Ring out a slowly dying cause,
    And ancient forms of party strife;
    Ring in the nobler modes of life,
With sweeter manners, purer laws.

Ring out the want, the care, the sin,
    The faithless coldness of the times;
    Ring out, ring out my mournful rhymes,
But ring the fuller minstrel in.   20

Ring out false pride in place and blood,
    The civic slander and the spite;
    Ring in the love of truth and right,
Ring in the common love of good.

Ring out old shapes of foul disease;
    Ring out the narrowing lust of gold;
    Ring out the thousand wars of old,
Ring in the thousand years of peace.

Ring in the valiant man and free,
    The larger heart, the kindlier hand;   30
    Ring out the darkness of the land,
Ring in the Christ that is to be.

115

Now fades the last long streak of snow,
    Now burgeons every maze of quick
    About the flowering squares, and thick
By ashen roots the violets blow.

Now rings the woodland loud and long,
    The distance takes a lovelier hue,
    And drown'd in yonder living blue
The lark becomes a sightless song.

Now dance the lights on lawn and lea,
    The flocks are whiter down the vale,   10
    And milkier every milky sail
On winding stream or distant sea;

Where now the seamew pipes, or dives
    In yonder greening gleam, and fly
    The happy birds, that change their sky
To build and brood; that live their lives

From land to land; and in my breast
    Spring wakens too; and my regret
    Becomes an April violet,
And buds and blossoms like the rest.   20

117

O days and hours, your work in this
    To hold me from my proper place,
    A little while from his embrace,
For fuller gain of after bliss:

That out of distance might ensue
    Desire of nearness doubly sweet;
    And unto meeting when we meet,
Delight a hundredfold accrue,

For every grain of sand that runs,
    And every span of shade that steals,   10

And every kiss of toothed wheels,
And all the courses of the suns.

123

There rolls the deep where grew the tree.
    O earth, what changes hast thou seen!
    There where the long street roars, hath been
The stillness of the central sea.

The hills are shadows, and they flow
    From form to form, and nothing stands;
    They melt like mist, the solid lands,
Like clouds they shape themselves and go.

But in my spirit will I dwell,
    And dream my dream, and hold it true;   10
    For tho' my lips may breathe adieu,
I cannot think the thing farewell.

129

Dear friend, far off, my lost desire,
    So far, so near in woe and weal;
    O loved the most, when most I feel
There is a lower and a higher;

Known and unknown; human, divine;
    Sweet human hand and lips and eye;
    Dear heavenly friend that canst not die,
Mine, mine, for ever, ever mine;

Strange friend, past, present, and to be;
    Love deeplier, darklier understood;   10
    Behold, I dream a dream of good,
And mingle all the world with thee.

from Ode on the Death of the Duke of Wellington

1

Bury the Great Duke
  With an empire's lamentation,
Let us bury the Great Duke
  To the noise of the mourning of a mighty nation,
Mourning when their leaders fall,
Warriors carry the warrior's pall,
And sorrow darkens hamlet and hall.

2

Where shall we lay the man whom we deplore?
Here, in streaming London's central roar.
Let the sound of those he wrought for,   10
And the feet of those he fought for,
Echo round his bones for evermore.

3

Lead out the pageant: sad and slow,
As fits an universal woe,
Let the long long procession go,
And let the sorrowing crowd about it grow,
And let the mournful martial music blow;
The last great Englishman is low.

8

Lo, the leader in these glorious wars
Now to glorious burial slowly borne,
Follow'd by the brave of other lands,
He, on whom from both her open hands
Lavish Honour shower'd all her stars,
And affluent Fortune emptied all her horn.

Yea, let all good things await
Him who cares not to be great,
But as he saves or serves the state.   200
Not once or twice in our rough island-story,
The path of duty was the way to glory:
He that walks it, only thirsting
For the right, and learns to deaden
Love of self, before his journey closes,
He shall find the stubborn thistle bursting
Into glossy purples, which outredden
All voluptuous garden-roses.
Not once or twice in our fair island-story,
The path of duty was the way to glory: 210
He, that ever following her commands,
On with toil of heart and knees and hands,
Thro' the long gorge to the far light has won
His path upward, and prevail'd,
Shall find the toppling crags of Duty scaled
Are close upon the shining table-lands
To which our God Himself is moon and sun.
Such was he: his work is done.
But while the races of mankind endure,
Let his great example stand   220
Colossal, seen of every land,
And keep the soldier firm, the statesman pure:
Till in all lands and thro' all human story
The path of duty be the way to glory:
And let the land whose hearths he saved from shame
For many and many an age proclaim
At civic revel and pomp and game,
And when the long-illumined cities flame,
Their ever-loyal iron leader's fame,
With honour, honour, honour, honour to him,   230
Eternal honour to his name.

9

Peace, his triumph will be sung
By some yet unmoulded tongue
Far on in summers that we shall not see:

Peace, it is a day of pain
For one about whose patriarchal knee
Late the little children clung:
O peace, it is a day of pain
For one, upon whose hand and heart and brain
Once the weight and fate of Europe hung.   240
Ours the pain, be his the gain!
More than is of man's degree
Must be with us, watching here
At this, our great solemnity.
Whom we see not we revere;
We revere, and we refrain
From talk of battles loud and vain,
And brawling memories all too free
For such a wise humility
As befits a solemn fane: 250
We revere, and while we hear
The tides of Music's golden sea
Setting toward eternity,
Uplifted high in heart and hope are we,
Until we doubt not that for one so true
There must be other nobler work to do
Than when he fought at Waterloo,
And Victor he must ever be.
For tho' the Giant Ages heave the hill
And break the shore, and evermore   260
Make and break, and work their will;
Tho' world on world in myriad myriads roll
Round us, each with different powers,
And other forms of life than ours,
What know we greater than the soul?
On God and Godlike men we build our trust.
Hush, the Dead March wails in the people's ears:
The dark crowd moves, and there are sobs and tears:
The black earth yawns: the mortal disappears;
Ashes to ashes, dust to dust;   270
He is gone who seem'd so great. –
Gone; but nothing can bereave him
Of the force he made his own
Being here, and we believe him

Something far advanced in State,
And that he wears a truer crown
Than any wreath that man can weave him.
Speak no more of his renown,
Lay your earthly fancies down,
And in the vast cathedral leave him.   280
God accept him, Christ receive him.

The Charge of the Light Brigade

Half a league, half a league,
  Half a league onward,
All in the valley of Death
  Rode the six hundred.
'Forward, the Light Brigade!
Charge for the guns!' he said:
Into the valley of Death
  Rode the six hundred.

'Forward, the Light Brigade!'
Was there a man dismay'd?   10
Not tho' the soldier knew
  Some one had blunder'd:
Their's not to make reply,
Their's not to reason why,
Their's but to do and die:
Into the valley of Death
  Rode the six hundred.

Cannon to right of them,
Cannon to left of them,
Cannon in front of them   20
  Volley'd and thunder'd;
Storm'd at with shot and shell,
Boldly they rode and well,
Into the jaws of Death,

Into the mouth of Hell
  Rode the six hundred.

Flash'd all their sabres bare,
Flash'd as they turn'd in air
Sabring the gunners there,
Charging an army, while   30
  All the world wonder'd:
Plunged in the battery smoke
Right thro' the line they broke;
Cossack and Russian
Reel'd from the sabre-stroke
  Shatter'd and sunder'd.
Then they rode back, but not
  Not the six hundred.

Cannon to right of them,
Cannon to left of them,   40
Cannon behind them
  Volley'd and thunder'd;
Storm'd at with shot and shell,
While horse and hero fell,
They that had fought so well
Came thro' the jaws of Death,
Back from the mouth of Hell,
All that was left of them,
  Left of six hundred.

When can their glory fade?   50
O the wild charge they made!
  All the world wonder'd.
Honour the charge they made!
Honour the Light Brigade,
  Noble six hundred!

from Maud: A Monodrama

PART I

1

I hate the dreadful hollow behind the little wood,
Its lips in the field above are dabbled with blood-red heath,
The red-ribb'd ledges drip with a silent horror of blood,
And Echo there, whatever is ask'd her, answers 'Death.'

For there in the ghastly pit long since a body was found,
His who had given me life – O father! O God! was it well? –
Mangled, and flatten'd, and crush'd, and dinted into the
      ground:
There yet lies the rock that fell with him when he fell.

Did he fling himself down? who knows? for a vast
      speculation had fail'd,
And ever he mutter'd and madden'd, and ever wann'd with
      despair,
And out he walk'd when the wind like a broken worldling
      wail'd,
And the flying gold of the ruin'd woodlands drove thro' the
      air.

I remember the time, for the roots of my hair were stirr'd
By a shuffled step, by a dead weight trail'd, by a whisper'd
      fright,
And my pulses closed their gates with a shock on my heart
      as I heard
The shrill-edged shriek of a mother divide the shuddering
      night.

Villainy somewhere! whose? One says, we are villains all.
Not he: his honest fame should at least by me be
      maintained:
But that old man, now lord of the broad estate and the Hall,

10

Dropt off gorged from a scheme that had left us flaccid and
    drain'd.   20

Why do they prate of the blessings of Peace? we have made
    them a curse,
Pickpockets, each hand lusting for all that is not its own;
And lust of gain, in the spirit of Cain, is it better or worse
Than the heart of the citizen hissing in war on his own
    hearthstone?

But these are the days of advance, the works of the men of
    mind,
When who but a fool would have faith in a tradesman's
    ware or his word?
Is it peace or war? Civil war, as I think, and that of a kind
The viler, as underhand, not openly bearing the sword.

Sooner or later I too may passively take the print
Of the golden age – why not? I have neither hope nor trust;   30
May make my heart as a millstone, set my face as a flint,
Cheat and be cheated, and die: who knows? we are ashes
    and dust.

Peace sitting under her olive, and slurring the days gone
    by,
When the poor are hovell'd and hustled together, each sex,
    like swine,
When only the ledger lives, and when only not all men lie;
Peace in her vineyard – yes! – but a company forges the
    wine.

And the vitriol madness flushes up in the ruffian's head,
Till the filthy by-lane rings to the yell of the trampled wife,
And chalk and alum and plaster are sold to the poor for
    bread,
And the spirit of murder works in the very means of life,   40

And Sleep must lie down arm'd, for the villainous centre-
    bits
Grind on the wakeful ear in the hush of the moonless
    nights,

While another is cheating the sick of a few last gasps, as he
    sits
To pestle a poison'd poison behind his crimson lights.

When a Mammonite mother kills her babe for a burial fee,
And Timour-Mammon grins on a pile of children's bones,
Is it peace or war? better, war! loud war by land and by sea,
War with a thousand battles, and shaking a hundred
    thrones.

For I trust if an enemy's fleet came yonder round by the
    hill,
And the rushing battle-bolt sang from the three-decker out
    of the foam,   50
That the smooth-faced snubnosed rogue would leap from
    his counter and till,
And strike, if he could, were it but with his cheating
    yardwand, home. —

What! am I raging alone as my father raged in his mood?
Must *I* too creep to the hollow and dash myself down and
    die
Rather than hold by the law that I made, nevermore to
    brood
On a horror of shatter'd limbs and a wretched swindler's
    lie?

Would there be sorrow for *me?* there was *love* in the
    passionate shriek,
Love for the silent thing that had made false haste to the
    grave –
Wrapt in a cloak, as I saw him, and thought he would rise
    and speak
And rave at the lie and the liar, ah God, as he used to rave.   60

I am sick of the Hall and the hill, I am sick of the moor and
    the main.
Why should I stay? can a sweeter chance ever come to me
    here?
O, having the nerves of motion as well as the nerves of
    pain,

Were it not wise If I fled from the place and the pit and the
    fear?

Workmen up at the Hall! – they are coming back from
    abroad;
The dark old place will be gilt by the touch of a millionaire:
I have heard, I know not whence, of the singular beauty of
    Maud;
I play'd with the girl when a child; she promised then to be
    fair.

Maud with her venturous climbings and tumbles and
    childish escapes,
Maud the delight of the village, the ringing joy of the Hall,   70
Maud with her sweet purse-mouth when my father dangled
    the grapes,
Maud the beloved of my mother, the moon-faced darling of
    all, –

What is she now? My dreams are bad. She may bring me a
    curse.
No, there is fatter game on the moor; she will let me alone.
Thanks, for the fiend best knows whether woman or man
    be the worse.
I will bury myself in myself, and the Devil may pipe to his
    own.

2

Long have I sigh'd for a calm: God grant I may find it at
    last!
It will never be broken by Maud, she has neither savour nor
    salt,
But a cold and clear-cut face, as I found when her carriage
    past,
Perfectly beautiful: let it be granted her: where is the fault?
All that I saw (for her eyes were downcast, not to be seen)
Faultily faultless, icily regular, splendidly null,
Dead perfection, no more; nothing more, if it had not been

For a chance of travel, a paleness, an hour's defect of the
    rose,
Or an underlip, you may call it a little too ripe, too full,
Or the least little delicate aquiline curve in a sensitive nose,   10
From which I escaped heart-free, with the least little touch
    of spleen.

3

Cold and clear-cut face, why come you so cruelly meek,
Breaking a slumber in which all spleenful folly was
    drown'd,
Pale with the golden beam of an eyelash dead on the cheek,
Passionless, pale, cold face, star-sweet on a gloom profound;
Womanlike, taking revenge too deep for a transient wrong
Done but in thought to your beauty, and ever as pale as
    before
Growing and fading and growing upon me without a
    sound,
Luminous, gemlike, ghostlike, deathlike, half the night long
Growing and fading and growing, till I could bear it no
    more,
But arose, and all by myself in my own dark garden
    ground,   10
Listening now to the tide in its broad-flung shipwrecking
    roar,
Now to the scream of a madden'd beach dragg'd down by
    the wave,
Walk'd in a wintry wind by a ghastly glimmer, and found
The shining daffodil dead, and Orion low in his grave.

10

Sick, am I sick of a jealous dread?
Was not one of the two at her side
This new-made lord, whose splendour plucks
The slavish hat from the villager's head?
Whose old grandfather has lately died,
Gone to a blacker pit, for whom
Grimy nakedness dragging his trucks

And laying his trams in a poison'd gloom
Wrought, till he crept from a gutted mine
Master of half a servile shire,   10
And left his coal all turn'd into gold
To a grandson, first of his noble line,
Rich in the grace all women desire,
Strong in the power that all men adore,
And simper and set their voices lower,
And soften as if to a girl, and hold
Awe-stricken breaths at a work divine,
Seeing his gewgaw castle shine,
New as his title, built last year,
There amid perky larches and pine,   20
And over the sullen-purple moor
(Look at it) pricking a cockney ear.

What, has he found my jewel out?
For one of the two that rode at her side
Bound for the Hall, I am sure was he:
Bound for the Hall, and I think for a bride.
Blithe would her brother's acceptance be.
Maud could be gracious too, no doubt
To a lord, a captain, a padded shape,
A bought commission, a waxen face,   30
A rabbit mouth that is ever agape –
Bought? what is it he cannot buy?
And therefore splenetic, personal, base,
A wounded thing with a rancorous cry,
At war with myself and a wretched race,
Sick, sick to the heart of life, am I.

Last week came one to the county town,
To preach our poor little army down,
And play the game of the despot kings,
Tho' the state has done it and thrice as well: 40
This broad-brimm'd hawker of holy things,
Whose ear is cramm'd with his cotton, and rings
Even in dreams to the chink of his pence,
This huckster put down war! can he tell
Whether war be a cause or a consequence?

Put down the passions that make earth Hell!
Down with ambition, avarice, pride,
Jealousy, down! cut off from the mind
The bitter springs of anger and fear;
Down too, down at your own fireside,   50
With the evil tongue and the evil ear,
For each is at war with mankind.

I wish I could hear again
The chivalrous battle-song
That she warbled alone in her joy!
I might persuade myself then
She would not do herself this great wrong,
To take a wanton dissolute boy
For a man and leader of men.

Ah God, for a man with heart, head, hand,   60
Like some of the simple great ones gone
For ever and ever by,
One still strong man in a blatant land,
Whatever they call him, what care I,
Aristocrat, democrat, autocrat – one
Who can rule and dare not lie.

And ah for a man to arise in me,
That the man I am may cease to be!

11

O let the solid ground
    Not fail beneath my feet
Before my life has found
    What some have found so sweet;
Then let come what come may,
What matter if I go mad,
I shall have had my day.

Let the sweet heavens endure,
    Not close and darken above me
Before I am quite quite sure   10

That there is one to love me;
Then let come what come may
To a life that has been so sad,
I shall have had my day.

22

Come into the garden, Maud,
    For the black bat, night, has flown,
Come into the garden, Maud,
    I am here at the gate alone;
And the woodbine spices are wafted abroad,
    And the musk of the rose is blown.

For a breeze of morning moves,
    And the planet of Love is on high,
Beginning to faint in the light that she loves
    On a bed of daffodil sky,   10
To faint in the light of the sun she loves,
    To faint in his light, and to die.

All night have the roses heard
    The flute, violin, bassoon;
All night has the casement jessamine stirr'd
    To the dancers dancing in tune;
Till a silence fell with the waking bird,
    And a hush with the setting moon.

I said to the lily, 'There is but one
    With whom she has heart to be gay.   20
When will the dancers leave her alone?
    She is weary of dance and play.'
Now half to the setting moon are gone,
    And half to the rising day;
Low on the sand and loud on the stone
    The last wheel echoes away.

I said to the rose, 'The brief night goes
    In babble and revel and wine.
O young lord-lover, what sighs are those,

For one that will never be thine?   30
But mine, but mine,' so I sware to the rose,
  'For ever and ever, mine.'

And the soul of the rose went into my blood,
  As the music clash'd in the hall;
And long by the garden lake I stood,
  For I heard your rivulet fall
From the lake to the meadow and on to the wood,
  Our wood, that is dearer than all;

From the meadow your walks have left so sweet
  That whenever a March-wind sighs   40
He sets the jewel-print of your feet
  In violets blue as your eyes,
To the woody hollows in which we meet
  And the valleys of Paradise.

The slender acacia would not shake
  One long milk-bloom on the tree;
The white lake-blossom fell into the lake
  As the pimpernel dozed on the lea;
But the rose was awake all night for your sake,
  Knowing your promise to me;   50
The lilies and roses were all awake,
  They sigh'd for the dawn and thee.

Queen rose of the rosebud garden of girls,
  Come hither, the dances are done,
In gloss of satin and glimmer of pearls,
  Queen lily and rose in one;
Shine out, little head, sunning over with curls,
  To the flowers, and be their sun.

There has fallen a splendid tear
  From the passion-flower at the gate.   60
She is coming, my dove, my dear;
  She is coming, my life, my fate;
The red rose cries, 'She is near, she is near;'
  And the white rose weeps, 'She is late;'

The larkspur listens, 'I hear, I hear;'
 And the lily whispers, 'I wait.'

She is coming, my own, my sweet;
 Were it ever so airy a tread,
My heart would hear her and beat,
 Were it earth in an earthy bed;   70
My dust would hear her and beat,
 Had I lain for a century dead;
Would start and tremble under her feet,
 And blossom in purple and red.

PART 2

1

'The fault was mine, the fault was mine' —
Why am I sitting here so stunn'd and still,
Plucking the harmless wild-flower on the hill? —
It is this guilty hand! —
And there rises ever a passionate cry
From underneath in the darkening land —
What is it, that has been done?
O dawn of Eden bright over earth and sky,
The fires of Hell brake out of thy rising sun,
The fires of Hell and of Hate;   10
For she, sweet soul, had hardly spoken a word,
When her brother ran in his rage to the gate,
He came with the babe-faced lord;
Heap'd on her terms of disgrace,
And while she wept, and I strove to be cool,
He fiercely gave me the lie,
Till I with as fierce an anger spoke,
And he struck me, madman, over the face,
Struck me before the languid fool,
Who was gaping and grinning by: 20
Struck for himself an evil stroke;
Wrought for his house an irredeemable woe;
For front to front in an hour we stood,

And a million horrible bellowing echoes broke
From the red-ribb'd hollow behind the wood,
And thunder'd up into Heaven the Christless code,
That must have life for a blow.
Ever and ever afresh they seem'd to grow.
Was it he lay there with a fading eye?
'The fault was mine,' he whisper'd, 'fly!'   30
Then glided out of the joyous wood
The ghastly Wraith of one that I know;
And there rang on a sudden a passionate cry,
A cry for a brother's blood:
It will ring in my heart and my ears, till I die, till I die.
Is it gone? my pulses beat —
What was it? a lying trick of the brain?
Yet I thought I saw her stand,
A shadow there at my feet,   40
High over the shadowy land.
It is gone; and the heavens fall in a gentle rain,
When they should burst and drown with deluging storms
The feeble vassals of wine and anger and lust,
The little hearts that know not how to forgive:
Arise, my God, and strike, for we hold Thee just,
Strike dead the whole weak race of venomous worms,
That sting each other here in the dust;
We are not worthy to live.

4

O that 'twere possible
After long grief and pain
To find the arms of my true love
Round me once again!

When I was wont to meet her
In the silent woody places
By the home that gave me birth,
We stood tranced in long embraces
Mixt with kisses sweeter sweeter
Than anything on earth.   10

A shadow flits before me,
Not thou, but like to thee:
Ah Christ, that it were possible
For one short hour to see
The souls we loved, that they might tell us
What and where they be.

It leads me forth at evening,
It lightly winds and steals
In a cold white robe before me,
When all my spirit reels   20
At the shouts, the leagues of lights,
And the roaring of the wheels.

Half the night I waste in sighs,
Half in dreams I sorrow after
The delight of early skies;
In a wakeful doze I sorrow
For the hand, the lips, the eyes,
For the meeting of the morrow,
The delight of happy laughter,
The delight of low replies.   30

'Tis a morning pure and sweet,
And a dewy splendour falls
On the little flower that clings
To the turrets and the walls;
'Tis a morning pure and sweet,
And the light and shadow fleet;
She is walking in the meadow,
And the woodland echo rings;
In a moment we shall meet;
She is singing in the meadow   40
And the rivulet at her feet
Ripples on in light and shadow
To the ballad that she sings.

Do I hear her sing as of old,
My bird with the shining head,
My own dove with the tender eye?

But there rings on a sudden a passionate cry,
There is some one dying or dead,
And a sullen thunder is roll'd;
For a tumult shakes the city,   50
And I wake, my dream is fled;
In the shuddering dawn, behold,
Without knowledge, without pity,
By the curtains of my bed
That abiding phantom cold.

Get thee hence, nor come again,
Mix not memory with doubt,
Pass, thou deathlike type of pain,
Pass and cease to move about!
'Tis the blot upon the brain   60
That *will* show itself without.

Then I rise, the eavedrops fall,
And the yellow vapours choke
The great city sounding wide;
The day comes, a dull red ball
Wrapt in drifts of lurid smoke
On the misty river-tide.

Thro' the hubbub of the market
I steal, a wasted frame,
It crosses here, it crosses there,   70
Thro' all that crowd confused and loud,
The shadow still the same;
And on my heavy eyelids
My anguish hangs like shame.

Alas for her that met me,
That heard me softly call,
Came glimmering thro' the laurels
At the quiet evenfall,
In the garden by the turrets
Of the old manorial hall.   80

Would the happy spirit descend,
From the realms of light and song,

In the chamber or the street,
As she looks among the blest,
Should I fear to greet my friend
Or to say 'Forgive the wrong,'
Or to ask her, 'Take me, sweet,
To the regions of thy rest'?

But the broad light glares and beats,
And the shadow flits and fleets   90
And will not let me be:
And I loathe the squares and streets,
And the faces that one meets,
Hearts with no love for me:
Always I long to creep
Into some still cavern deep,
There to weep, and weep, and weep
My whole soul out to thee.

5

Dead, long dead,
Long dead!
And my heart is a handful of dust,
And the wheels go over my head,
And my bones are shaken with pain,
For into a shallow grave they are thrust,
Only a yard beneath the street,
And the hoofs of the horses beat, beat,
The hoofs of the horses beat,
Beat into my scalp and my brain,   10
With never an end to the stream of passing feet,
Driving, hurrying, marrying, burying,
Clamour and rumble, and ringing and clatter,
And here beneath it is all as bad,
For I thought the dead had peace, but it is not so;
To have no peace in the grave, is that not sad?
But up and down and to and fro,
Ever about me the dead men go;

And then to hear a dead man chatter
Is enough to drive one mad.   20

Wretchedest age, since Time began,
They cannot even bury a man;
And tho' we paid our tithes in the days that are gone,
Not a bell was rung, not a prayer was read;
It is that which makes us loud in the world of the dead;
There is none that does his work, not one;
A touch of their office might have sufficed,
But the churchmen fain would kill their church,
As the churches have kill'd their Christ.

See, there is one of us sobbing,   30
No limit to his distress;
And another, a lord of all things, praying
To his own great self, as I guess;
And another, a statesman there, betraying
His party-secret, fool, to the press;
And yonder a vile physician, blabbing
The case of his patient – all for what?
To tickle the maggot born in an empty head,
And wheedle a world that loves him not,
For it is but a world of the dead.   40

Nothing but idiot gabble!
For the prophecy given of old
And then not understood,
Has come to pass as foretold;
Not let any man think for the public good,
But babble, merely for babble.
For I never whisper'd a private affair
Within the hearing of cat or mouse,
No, not to myself in the closet alone,
But I heard it shouted at once from the top of the house;   50
Everything came to be known.
Who told *him* we were there?

Not that gray old wolf, for he came not back
From the wilderness, full of wolves, where he used to lie;

He has gathered the bones for his o'ergrown whelp to crack;
Crack them now for yourself, and howl, and die.

Prophet, curse me the blabbing lip,
And curse me the British vermin, the rat;
I know not whether he came in the Hanover ship,
But I know that he lies and listens mute   60
In an ancient mansion's crannies and holes:
Arsenic, arsenic, sure, would do it,
Except that now we poison our babes, poor souls!
It is all used up for that.

Tell him now: she is standing here at my head;
Not beautiful now, not even kind;
He may take her now; for she never speaks her mind,
But is ever the one thing silent here.
She is not *of* us, as I divine;
She comes from another stiller world of the dead,   70
Stiller, not fairer than mine.

But I know where a garden grows,
Fairer than aught in the world beside,
All made up of the lily and rose
That blow by night, when the season is good,
To the sound of dancing music and flutes:
It is only flowers, they had no fruits,
And I almost fear they are not roses, but blood;
For the keeper was one, so full of pride,
He linkt a dead man there to a spectral bride;   80
For he, if he had not been a Sultan of brutes,
Would he have that hole in his side?

But what will the old man say?
He laid a cruel snare in a pit
To catch a friend of mine one stormy day;
Yet now I could even weep to think of it;
For what will the old man say
When he comes to the second corpse in the pit?

Friend, to be struck by the public foe,
Then to strike him and lay him low,   90
That were a public merit, far,
Whatever the Quaker holds, from sin;
But the red life spilt for a private blow –
I swear to you, lawful and lawless war
Are scarcely even akin.

O me, why have they not buried me deep enough?
Is it kind to have made me a grave so rough,
Me, that was never a quiet sleeper?
Maybe still I am but half-dead;
Then I cannot be wholly dumb;   100
I will cry to the steps above my head
And somebody, surely, some kind heart will come
To bury me, bury me
Deeper, ever so little deeper.

PART 3

6

My life has crept so long on a broken wing
Thro' cells of madness, haunts of horror and fear,
That I come to be grateful at last for a little thing:
My mood is changed, for it fell at a time of year
When the face of night is fair on the dewy downs,
And the shining daffodil dies, and the Charioteer
And starry Gemini hang like glorious crowns
Over Orion's grave low down in the west,
That like a silent lightning under the stars
She seem'd to divide in a dream from a band of the blest,   10
And spoke of a hope for the world in the coming wars –
'And in that hope, dear soul, let trouble have rest,
Knowing I tarry for thee,' and pointed to Mars
As he glow'd like a ruddy shield on the Lion's breast.

And it was but a dream, yet it yielded a dear delight
To have look'd, tho' but in a dream, upon eyes so fair,

That had been in a weary world my one thing bright;
And it was but a dream, yet it lighten'd my despair
When I thought that a war would arise in defence of the right,
That an iron tyranny now should bend or cease,   20
The glory of manhood stand on his ancient height,
Nor Britain's one sole God be the millionaire:
No more shall commerce be all in all, and Peace
Pipe on her pastoral hillock a languid note,
And watch her harvest ripen, her herd increase,
Nor the cannon-bullet rust on a slothful shore,
And the cobweb woven across the cannon's throat
Shall shake its threaded tears in the wind no more.

And as months ran on and rumour of battle grew,
'It is time, it is time, O passionate heart,' said I   30
(For I cleaved to a cause that I felt to be pure and true),
'It is time, O passionate heart and morbid eye,
That old hysterical mock-disease should die.'
And I stood on a giant deck and mix'd my breath
With a loyal people shouting a battle cry,
Till I saw the dreary phantom arise and fly
Far into the North, and battle, and seas of death.

Let it go or stay, so I wake to the higher aims
Of a land that has lost for a little her lust of gold,
And love of a peace that was full of wrongs and shames,   40
Horrible, hateful, monstrous, not to be told;
And hail once more to the banner of battle unroll'd!
Tho' many a light shall darken, and many shall weep
For those that are crush'd in the clash of jarring claims,
Yet God's just wrath shall be wreak'd on a giant liar;
And many a darkness into the light shall leap,
And shine in the sudden making of splendid names,
And noble thought be freër under the sun,
And the heart of a people beat with one desire;
For the peace, that I deem'd no peace, is over and done,   50
And now by the side of the Black and the Baltic deep,
And deathful-grinning mouths of the fortress, flames
The blood-red blossom of war with a heart of fire.

Let it flame or fade, and the war roll down like a wind,
We have proved we have hearts in a cause, we are noble still,
And myself have awaked, as it seems, to the better mind;
It is better to fight for the good than to rail at the ill;
I have felt with my native land, I am one with my kind,
I embrace the purpose of God, and the doom assign'd.

Tithonus

The woods decay, the woods decay and fall,
The vapours weep their burthen to the ground,
Man comes and tills the field and lies beneath,
And after many a summer dies the swan.
Me only cruel immortality
Consumes: I wither slowly in thine arms,
Here at the quiet limit of the world,
A white-hair'd shadow roaming like a dream
The ever-silent spaces of the East,
Far-folded mists, and gleaming halls of morn.   10

    Alas! for this gray shadow, once a man –
So glorious in his beauty and thy choice,
Who madest him thy chosen, that he seem'd
To his great heart none other than a God!
I ask'd thee, 'Give me immortality.'
Then didst thou grant mine asking with a smile,
Like wealthy men who care not how they give.
But thy strong Hours indignant work'd their wills,
And beat me down and marr'd and wasted me,
And tho' they could not end me, left me maim'd   20
To dwell in presence of immortal youth,
Immortal age beside immortal youth,
And all I was, in ashes. Can thy love,
Thy beauty, make amends, tho' even now,

Close over us, the silver star, thy guide,
Shines in those tremulous eyes that fill with tears
To hear me? Let me go: take back thy gift:
Why should a man desire in any way
To vary from the kindly race of men,
Or pass beyond the goal of ordinance   30
Where all should pause, as is most meet for all?

A soft air fans the cloud apart; there comes
A glimpse of that dark world where I was born.
Once more the old mysterious glimmer steals
From thy pure brows, and from thy shoulders pure,
And bosom beating with a heart renew'd.
Thy cheek begins to redden thro' the gloom,
Thy sweet eyes brighten slowly close to mine,
Ere yet they blind the stars, and the wild team
Which love thee, yearning for thy yoke, arise,   40
And shake the darkness from their loosen'd manes,
And beat the twilight into flakes of fire.

Lo! ever thus thou growest beautiful
In silence, then before thine answer given
Departest, and thy tears are on my cheek.

Why wilt thou ever scare me with thy tears,
And make me tremble lest a saying learnt,
In days far-off, on that dark earth, be true?
'The Gods themselves cannot recall their gifts.'

Ay me! ay me! with what another heart   50
In days far-off, and with what other eyes
I used to watch – if I be he that watch'd –
The lucid outline forming round thee; saw
The dim curls kindle into sunny rings;
Changed with thy mystic change, and felt my blood
Glow with the glow that slowly crimson'd all
Thy presence and thy portals, while I lay,
Mouth, forehead, eyelids, growing dewy-warm
With kisses balmier than half-opening buds
Of April, and could hear the lips that kiss'd   60
Whispering I knew not what of wild and sweet,

Like that strange song I heard Apollo sing,
While Ilion like a mist rose into towers.

Yet hold me not for ever in thine East:
How can my nature longer mix with thine?
Coldly thy rosy shadows bathe me, cold
Are all thy lights, and cold my wrinkled feet
Upon thy glimmering thresholds, when the steam
Floats up from those dim fields about the homes
Of happy men that have the power to die,   70
And grassy barrows of the happier dead.
Release me, and restore me to the ground;
Thou seëst all things, thou wilt see my grave:
Thou wilt renew thy beauty morn by morn;
I earth in earth forget these empty courts,
And thee returning on thy silver wheels.

Northern Farmer

New Style

Dosn't thou 'ear my 'erse's legs, as they canters awaäy?
Proputty, proputty, proputty – that's what I 'ears 'em saäy.
Proputty, proputty, proputty – Sam, thou's an ass for thy
    paaïns:
Theer's moor sense i' one o' 'is legs nor in all thy braaïns.

Woä – theer's a craw to pluck wi' tha, Sam: yon's parson's
    'ouse –
Dosn't thou knaw that a man mun be eäther a man or a
    mouse?
Time to think on it then; for thou'll be twenty to weeäk.
Proputty, proputty – woä then woä – let ma 'ear mysén
    speäk.

Me an' thy muther, Sammy, 'as beän a-talkin' o' thee;
Thou's beän talkin' to muther, an' she beän a tellin' it me.   10

Thou'll not marry for munny – thou's sweet upo' parson's
    lass –
Noä – thou'll marry for luvv – an' we boäth on us thinks
    tha an ass.

Seeä'd her todaäy goä by – Saäint's-daäy – they was
    ringing the bells.
She's a beauty thou thinks – an' soä is scoors o' gells,
Them as 'as munny an' all – wot's a beauty? – the flower as
    blaws.
But proputty, proputty sticks, an' proputty, proputty graws.

Do'ant be stunt: taäke time: I knaws what maäkes tha sa
    mad.
Warn't I craäzed fur the lasses mysén when I wur a lad?
But I knaw'd a Quaäker feller as often 'as towd ma this:
'Doänt thou marry for munny, but goä wheer munny is!'   20

An' I went wheer munny war: an' thy muther coom to
    'and,
Wi' lots o' munny laaïd by, an' a nicetish bit o' land.
Maäybe she warn't a beauty: – I niver give it a thowt –
But warn't she as good to cuddle an' kiss as a lass as 'ant
    nowt?

Parson's lass 'ant nowt, an' she weänt 'a nowt when 'e's
    deäd,
Mun be a guvness, lad, or summut, and addle her breäd:
Why? fur 'e's nobbut a curate, an' weänt niver git hissen
    clear,
An' 'e maäde the bed as 'e ligs on afoor 'e coom'd to the
    shere.

An' thin 'e coom'd to the parish wi' lots o' Varsity debt,
Stook to his taaïl they did, an' 'e 'ant got shut on 'em yet.   30
An' 'e ligs on 'is back i' the grip, wi' noän to lend 'im a shuvv,
Woorse nor a far-welter'd yowe: fur, Sammy, 'e married fur luvv.

Luvv? what's luvv? thou can luvv thy lass an' 'er munny too,
Maäkin' 'em goä togither as they've good right to do.

Could'n I luvv thy muther by cause o' 'er munny laaïd by?
Naäy – fur I luvv'd 'er a vast sight moor fur it: reäson why.

Ay an' thy muther says thou wants to marry the lass,
Cooms of a gentleman burn: an' we boäth on us thinks tha an
    ass.
Woä then, proputty, wiltha? – an ass as near as mays nowt –
Woä then, wiltha? dangtha! – the bees is as fell as owt.   40

Breäk me a bit o' the esh for his 'eäd, lad, out o' the fence!
Gentleman burn! what's gentleman burn? is it shillins an'
    pence?
Proputty, proputty's ivrything 'ere, an', Sammy, I'm blest
If it isn't the saäme oop yonder, fur them as 'as it's the best.

Tis'n them as 'as munny as breäks into 'ouses an' steäls,
Them as 'as coäts to their backs an' taäkes their regular
    meäls.
Noä, but it's them as niver knaws wheer a meäl's to be 'ad.
Taäke my word for it, Sammy, the poor in a loomp is bad.

Them or thir feythers, tha sees, mun 'a beän a laäzy lot,
Fur work mun 'a gone to the gittin' whiniver munny was
    got.   50
Feyther 'ad ammost nowt; leästways 'is munny was 'id.
But 'e tued an' moil'd 'issén deäd, an 'e died a good un, 'e
    did.

Loook thou theer wheer Wrigglesby beck cooms out by the
    'ill!
Feyther run oop to the farm, an' I runs oop to the mill;
An' I'll run oop to the brig, an' that thou'll live to see;
And if thou marries a good un I'll leäve the land to thee.

Thim's my noätions, Sammy, wheerby I means to stick;
But if thou marries a bad un, I'll leäve the land to Dick. –
Coom oop, proputty, proputty – that's what I 'ears 'im saäy
Proputty, proputty, proputty – canter an' canter awaäy.   60

from Merlin and Vivien

And after that, she set herself to gain
Him, the most famous man of all those times,
Merlin, who knew the range of all their arts,
Had built the King his havens, ships, and halls,
Was also Bard, and knew the starry heavens;
The people called him Wizard; whom at first
She play'd about with slight and sprightly talk,
And vivid smiles, and faintly-venom'd points   170
Of slander, glancing here and gazing there;
And yielding to his kindlier moods, the Seer
Would watch her at her petulance, and play,
Even when they seem'd unloveable, and laugh
As those that watch a kitten; thus he grew
Tolerant of what he half disdain'd, and she,
Perceiving that she was but half disdain'd,
Began to break her sports with graver fits,
Turn red or pale, would often when they met
Sigh fully, or all-silent gaze upon him   180
With such a fixt devotion, that the old man,
Tho' doubtful, felt the flattery, and at times
Would flatter his own wish in age for love,
And half believe her true: for thus at times
He waver'd; but that other clung to him,
Fixt in her will, and so the seasons went.
　　Then fell on Merlin a great melancholy;
He walk'd with dreams and darkness, and he found
A doom that ever poised itself to fall,
An ever-moaning battle in the mist,   190
World-war of dying flesh against the life,
Death in all life and lying in all love,
The meanest having power upon the highest,
And the high purpose broken by the worm.
　　So leaving Arthur's court he gain'd the beach;
There found a little boat, and stept into it;
And Vivien follow'd, but he mark'd her not.
She took the helm and he the sail; the boat
Drave with a sudden wind across the deeps,

And touching Breton sands, they disembark'd. 200
And then she follow'd Merlin all the way,
Even to the wild woods of Broceliande.
For Merlin once had told her of a charm,
The which if any wrought on anyone
With woven paces and with waving arms,
The man so wrought on ever seem'd to lie
Closed in the four walls of a hollow tower,
From which was no escape for evermore;
And none could find that man for evermore,
Nor could he see but him who wrought the charm 210
Coming and going, and he lay as dead
And lost to life and use and name and fame.
And Vivien ever sought to work the charm
Upon the great Enchanter of the Time,
As fancying that her glory would be great
According to his greatness whom she quench'd.
   There lay she all her length and kiss'd his feet,
As if in deepest reverence and in love.
A twist of gold was round her hair; a robe
Of samite without price, that more exprest 220
Than hid her, clung about her lissome limbs,
In colour like the satin-shining palm
On sallows in the windy gleams of March:
And while she kiss'd them, crying, 'Trample me,
Dear feet, that I have follow'd thro' the world,
And I will pay you worship; tread me down
And I will kiss you for it;' he was mute:
So dark a forethought roll'd about his brain,
As on a dull day in an Ocean cave
The blind wave feeling round his long sea-hall 230
In silence: wherefore, when she lifted up
A face of sad appeal, and spake and said,
'O Merlin, do ye love me?' and again,
'O Merlin, do ye love me?' and once more,
'Great Master, do ye love me?' he was mute.
And lissome Vivien, holding by his heel,
Writhed toward him, slided up his knee and sat,
Behind his ankle twined her hollow feet
Together, curved an arm about his neck,

Clung like a snake; and letting her left hand   240
Droop from his mighty shoulder, as a leaf,
Made with her right a comb of pearl to part
The lists of such a beard as youth gone out
Had left in ashes: then he spoke and said,
Not looking at her, 'Who are wise in love
Love most, say least,' and Vivien answered quick,
'I saw the little elf-god eyeless once
In Arthur's arras hall at Camelot:
But neither eyes nor tongue – O stupid child!
Yet you are wise who say it; let me think   250
Silence is wisdom: I am silent then,
And ask no kiss;' then adding all at once,
'And lo, I clothe myself with wisdom,' drew
The vast and shaggy mantle of his beard
Across her neck and bosom to her knee,
And call'd herself a gilded summer fly
Caught in a great old tyrant spider's web,
Who meant to eat her up in that wild wood
Without one word. So Vivien call'd herself,
But rather seem'd a lovely baleful star   260
Veiled in gray vapour; till he sadly smiled:
'To what request for what strange boon,' he said,
'Are these your pretty tricks and fooleries,
O Vivien, the preamble? yet my thanks,
For these have broken up my melancholy.'

    And Vivien answer'd smiling saucily,
'What, O my Master, have ye found your voice?
I bid the stranger welcome. Thanks at last!
But yesterday you never opened lip,
Except indeed to drink: no cup had we: 270
In mine own lady palms I cull'd the spring
That gather'd trickling dropwise from the cleft,
And made a pretty cup of both my hands
And offer'd you it kneeling: then you drank
And knew no more, nor gave me one poor word;
O no more thanks than might a goat have given
With no more sign of reverence than a beard.
And when we halted at that other well,
And I was faint to swooning, and you lay

Foot-gilt with all the blossom-dust of those   280
Deep meadows we had traversed, did you know
That Vivien bathed your feet before her own?
And yet no thanks: and all thro' this wild wood
And all this morning when I fondled you:
Boon, ay, there was a boon, one not so strange –
How had I wrong'd you? surely ye are wise,
But such a silence is more wise than kind.'

And Merlin lock'd his hand in hers and said:
'O did ye never lie upon the shore,
And watch the curl'd white of the coming wave   290
Glass'd in the slippery sand before it breaks?
Even such a wave, but not so pleasurable,
Dark in the glass of some presageful mood,
Had I for three days seen, ready to fall.
And then I rose and fled from Arthur's court
To break the mood. You follow'd me unask'd;
And when I look'd, and saw you following still,
My mind involved yourself the nearest thing
In that mind-mist: for shall I tell you truth?
You seem'd that wave about to break upon me   300
And sweep me from my hold upon the world,
My use and name and fame. Your pardon, child.
Your pretty sports have brighten'd all again.
And ask your boon, for boon I owe you thrice,
Once for wrong done you by confusion, next
For thanks it seems till now neglected, last
For these your dainty gambols: wherefore ask;
And take this boon so strange and not so strange.'

And Vivien answer'd smiling mournfully:
'O not so strange as my long asking it,   310
Not yet so strange as you yourself are strange,
Nor half so strange as that dark mood of yours.
I ever fear'd ye were not wholly mine;
And see, yourself have own'd ye did me wrong.
The people call you prophet: let it be:
But not of those that can expound themselves.
Take Vivien for expounder; she will call
That three-days-long presageful gloom of yours

No presage, but the same mistrustful mood
That makes you seem less noble than yourself,   320
Whenever I have ask'd this very boon,
Now ask'd again: for see you not, dear love,
That such a mood as that, which lately gloom'd
Your fancy when ye saw me following you,
Must make me fear still more you are not mine,
Must make me yearn still more to prove you mine,
And make me wish still more to learn this charm
Of woven paces and of waving hands,
As proof of trust. O Merlin, teach it me.
The charm so taught will charm us both to rest.   330
For, grant me some slight power upon your fate,
I, feeling that you felt me worthy trust,
Should rest and let you rest, knowing you mine.
And therefore be as great as ye are named,
Not muffled round with selfish reticence.
How hard you look and how denyingly!
O, if you think this wickedness in me,
That I should prove it on you unawares,
That makes me passing wrathful; then our bond
Had best be loosed for ever: but think or not,   340
By Heaven that hears I tell you the clean truth,
As clean as blood of babes, as white as milk:
O Merlin, may this earth, if every I,
If these unwitty wandering wits of mine,
Even in the jumbled rubbish of a dream,
Have tript on such conjectural treachery –
May this hard earth cleave to the Nadir hell
Down, down, and close again, and nip me flat,
If I be such a traitress. Yield my boon,
Till which I scarce can yield you all I am;   350
And grant my re-reiterated wish,
The great proof of your love: because I think,
However wise, ye hardly know me yet.'

    And Merlin loosed his hand from hers and said,
'I never was less wise, however wise,
Too curious Vivien, tho' you talk of trust,
Than when I told you first of such a charm.

Yea, if ye talk of trust I tell you this,
Too much I trusted when I told you that,
And stirr'd this vice in you which ruin'd man   360
Thro' woman the first hour; for howsoe'er
In children a great curiousness be well,
Who have to learn themselves and all the world,
In you, that are no child, for still I find
Your face is practised when I spell the lines,
I call it, – well, I will not call it vice:
But since you name yourself the summer fly,
I well could wish a cobweb for the gnat,
That settles, beaten back, and beaten back
Settles, till one could yield for weariness: 370
But since I will not yield to give you power
Upon my life and use and name and fame,
Why will ye never ask some other boon?
Yea, by God's rood, I trusted you too much.'

And Vivien, like the tenderest-hearted maid
That ever bided tryst at village stile,
Made answer, either eyelid wet with tears:
'Nay, Master, be not wrathful with your maid;
Caress her: let her feel herself forgiven
Who feels no heart to ask another boon.   380
I think ye hardly know the tender rhyme
Of "trust me not at all or all in all."
I heard the great Sir Lancelot sing it once,
And it shall answer for me. Listen to it.

"In Love, if Love be Love, if Love be ours,
Faith and unfaith can ne'er be equal powers:
Unfaith in aught is want of faith in all.

"It is the little rift within the lute,
That by and by will make the music mute,
And ever widening slowly silence all.   390

"The little rift within the lover's lute
Or little pitted speck in garnered fruit,
That rotting inward slowly moulders all.

"It is not worth the keeping: let it go:
But shall it? answer, darling, answer, no.
And trust me not at all or all in all."

O Master, do ye love my tender rhyme?'

And Merlin look'd and half believed her true,
So tender was her voice, so fair her face,
So sweetly gleam'd her eyes behind her tears   400
Like sunlight on the plain behind a shower[.]

To E. FitzGerald

Old Fitz, who from your suburb grange,
    Where once I tarried for a while,
Glance at the wheeling Orb of change,
    And greet it with a kindly smile;
Whom yet I see as there you sit
    Beneath your sheltering garden-tree,
And while your doves about you flit,
    And plant on shoulder, hand and knee,
Or on your head their rosy feet,
    As if they knew your diet spares   10
Whatever moved in that full sheet
    Let down to Peter at his prayers;
Who live on milk and meal and grass;
    And once for ten long weeks I tried
Your table of Pythagoras,
    And seem'd at first 'a thing enskied'
(As Shakespeare has it) airy-light
    To float above the ways of men,
Then fell from that half-spiritual height
    Chill'd, till I tasted flesh again   20
One night when earth was winter-black,
    And all the heavens flash'd in frost;
And on me, half-asleep, came back

That wholesome heat the blood had lost,
And set me climbing icy capes
    And glaciers, over which there roll'd
To meet me long-arm'd vines with grapes
    Of Eshcol hugeness; for the cold
Without, and warmth within me, wrought
    To mould the dream; but none can say   30
That Lenten fare makes Lenten thought,
    Who reads your golden Eastern lay,
Than which I know no version done
    In English more divinely well;
A planet equal to the sun
    Which cast it, that large infidel
Your Omar; and your Omar drew
    Full-handed plaudits from our best
In modern letters, and from two,
    Old friends outvaluing all the rest,   40
Two voices heard on earth no more;
    But we old friends are still alive,
And I am nearing seventy-four,
    While you have touch'd at seventy-five,
And so I send a birthday line
    Of greeting; and my son, who dipt
In some forgotten book of mine
    With sallow scraps of manuscript,
And dating many a year ago,
    Has hit on this, which you will take   50
My Fitz, and welcome, as I know
    Less for its own than for the sake
Of one recalling gracious times,
    When, in our younger London days,
You found some merit in my rhymes,
    And I more pleasure in your praise.

Crossing The Bar

Sunset and evening star,
   And one clear call for me!
And may there be no moaning of the bar,
   When I put out to sea,

But such a tide as moving seems asleep,
   Too full for sound and foam,
When that which drew from out the boundless deep
   Turns again home.

Twilight and evening bell,
   And after that the dark!   10
And may there be no sadness of farewell,
   When I embark;

For tho' from out our bourne of Time and Place
   The flood may bear me far,
I hope to see my Pilot face to face
   When I have crost the bar.

June Bracken and Heather

To –

There on the top of the down,
The wild heather round me and over me June's high blue,
When I looked at the bracken so bright and the heather so
   brown,
I thought to myself I would offer this book to you,
This, and my love together,
To you that are seventy-seven,

With a faith as clear as the heights of the June-blue heaven,
And a fancy as summer-new
As the green of the bracken amid the gloom of the heather.

Notes

(Poems are printed in the order in which they were completed. *1830*, *1833*, *1842*, etc. refer to the dates of first publication. For details see Chronology.)

The Outcast Written probably in 1826; first published 1931.

Mariana (*1830*) Tennyson imagines the thoughts and feelings of Shakespeare's Mariana, abandoned by her betrothed, Angelo, and living in a remote grange (*Measure for Measure*). **40 marish-mosses**: lumps of marsh-moss floating on the water. **54 cell**: the cave of Aeolus, the god of the winds.

The Lady of Shalott (*1832*) The poem questions life in terms of an opposition between art and reality and inspired a number of contemporary painters. Of lines 69–72 Tennyson wrote, 'The new-born love for something, for some one in the wide world from which she has been so long secluded, takes her out of the region of shadows into that of realities.' **5 Camelot**: legendary capital of King Arthur's kingdom. **22 shallop**: small sailing or rowing boat. **46 mirror**: a mirror was set beside the tapestry so that the worker could see the pattern the right way round. **56 pad**: easy-paced horse. **84 Galaxy**: the Milky Way. **87 blazon'd baldric**: heraldically decorated shoulder-belt.

The Lotos-eaters (*1832*) In Homer's *Odyssey*, ix, Odysseus tells how he landed in the country of the Lotos-Eaters, where the natives gave the members of his reconnaissance party some lotos to taste. As soon as they had eaten it, they lost all idea of reporting back and wished merely to linger. Odysseus had to force them back to the ships. **1 he**: Odysseus. **11 lawn**: a kind of fine linen. **23 galingale**: an aromatic herb. **44 island home**: Ithaca.

Ulysses (*1842*) Written in October 1833, shortly after Tennyson learned of Hallam's death. Ulysses (Odysseus) is about to leave his island kingdom of Ithaca to his prudent son Telemachus and set out on a great adventure which he hopes may even reunite him with his dead comrade in the Trojan War, Achilles. Tennyson had read in Homer's *Odyssey*, xi, and Dante's *Inferno*, xxvi, Teiresias's prophecy of Odysseus's last, fatal voyage. **3 mete**:

administer. **4 Unequal**: 'not affecting all in the same manner or degree' (Tennyson). **10 rainy Hyades**: the rising of these five stars was thought to bring stormy weather. **63 Happy Isles**: Isles of the Blest, imagined as lying beyond the Straits of Gibraltar.

Morte d'Arthur (*1842*) Written following Hallam's death. It subsequently developed into 'The Passing of Arthur' (1869), finally part of *Idylls of the King*. Tennyson drew his material mainly from Malory's *Le Morte Darthur*. **4 Lyonnesse**: 'the country of legend that lay between Cornwall and the Scilly Islands' (Tennyson). **23 Merlin**: magician and companion of King Arthur. **110 conceit**: fancy. **139 streamer**: Aurora Borealis or northern lights. **140 moving isles of winter shock**: icebergs collide. **198 Three Queens**: in Malory, one is Arthur's sister, Morgan le Fay, and the other two are the Queens of Northgalis and of the Waste Lands. According to Tennyson, 'some say that the three Queens are Faith, Hope and Charity . . .' **215–16 greaves and cuisses dash'd with drops Of onset**: shin and thigh armour spattered with blood from combat. **232 light**: Star of Bethlehem. **234 ROUND TABLE**: Arthur's Knights, collectively, as well as the table itself. **242 one good custom**: 'e.g. chivalry' (Tennyson). **259 Avilion**: usually Avalon, the Isle of the Blest in Celtic mythology.

'Break, Break, Break . . .' (*1842*) Probably written in spring 1834, after Hallam's death.

Locksley Hall (*1842*) Written 1837–8, about the time when Rosa Baring's marriage was being arranged. The speaker denounces the materialism which he thinks has cost him the woman he loves and determines to commit himself to the progressive politics of the day. In subject and feeling the poem anticipates *Maud*. **8 Orion**: a constellation. **9 Pleiads**: seven stars within the constellation Taurus. **19 iris**: range of feather colours, especially on the neck, which brighten in the mating season. **41 fathoms**: realises. **75 the poet**: Dante (*Inferno*, v). **79 he**: Amy's husband. **104 laid**: in keeping with the belief that gunfire calms the waves. **121–4 magic sails . . . airy navies**: balloons. **138 process of the suns**: passage of the years. **150 motions**: feelings. **155 Mahratta-battle**: Britain had been involved in a series of wars against the Mahrattas of northern India from 1779 to 1818. **180 Joshua's moon**: in Joshua x.12–13, God allows him to halt the sun and moon. **182 ringing grooves**: Tennyson composed this line after his first railway ride. He wrongly assumed that the wheels ran in grooves. **184 Cathay**: China.

The Golden Year (*1846*) Written at Llanberis, Snowdonia, probably in 1839. The idea of the 'golden year' is based on a classical conception of a new era, as in Virgil's *Eclogue iv*. **12–13 daughters ... all**: cf. Proverbs xxx.15: 'The horse-leech [i.e. horse-doctor] hath two daughters, crying, Give, give.' **65 happy season**: the classical conception of the golden age, at the beginning of the world.

From *The Princess* (*1847*; extensively revised for subsequent editions) The poem, by far the longest Tennyson had written so far, is a debate about the education of women. The three lyrics 'Tears, idle tears', 'Now sleeps the crimson petal', and 'Come down, O maid', formed part of the whole poem from the start; the song, 'The splendour falls', was written after 1847 and published in 1850.

The splendour falls 'Written after hearing the echoes at Killarney in 1848. When I was there I heard a bugle blown beneath the "Eagle's Nest," and eight distinct echoes' (Tennyson). **1 splendour**: of the sunset. **10 Elfland**: Fairyland.

Tears, idle tears Tennyson conceived this song during an autumn visit to Tintern Abbey.

Now sleeps the crimson petal Influenced in form and imagery by Persian poetry. **7 Danaë**: 'Zeus came down to Danaë when shut up in the tower in a shower of golden stars' (Tennyson).

Come down, O maid Written in Switzerland. **12 foxlike in the vine**: stealing the grapes. Cf. Song of Solomon ii.15. **13 silver horns**: snow-clad peaks. **17 dusky**: in contrast with the snows around. **25 azure pillars**: of rising smoke.

From *In Memoriam A.H.H.* (*1850*) Tennyson's memorial to Hallam, written as a collection of separate 'elegies' over seventeen years. Tennyson wrote that ' "I" is not always the author speaking of himself, but the voice of the human race speaking through him.' **1, 1 him**: 'Goethe's creed ... "from changes to higher changes" ' (Tennyson). **1, 8 far-off interest of tears**: future recompense for present grief. **2, 15 fail from out**: slip away from. **5, 9 weeds**: clothes; perhaps mourning clothes. **7, 1 house**: '67 Wimpole Street' (Tennyson) – Hallam's London home. **21, 15–16 civil power**: probably an allusion to Chartist agitation. **39** written in 1868, a late addition to *In Memoriam*. **39, 3 fruitful cloud and living smoke**: 'The yew, when flowering, in a wind or if struck sends up its pollen like smoke' (Tennyson). **50** Addressed to Hallam. **50, 8 slinging flame**: the Furies carried torches. **54, 18 infant**: Latin *infans* meaning, among other things, 'unable to speak'. **55, 56** In writing of nature's indifference to the individual and to the species ('red in tooth and claw'), and to evidence 'seal'd within the iron hills', Tennyson recalls Lyell's *Principles of Geology* (1830–3), which he read in 1837. **56, 22 Dragons of the prime**: prehistoric monsters. **56, 28 behind the veil**: the veil of truth. **77, 7 maiden's locks**: paper rolls were used in curling hair. **93, 12 Tenfold-complicated**: an allusion to Dante's image of the ten concentric spheres of heaven (*Paradiso*, xxviii). **96, 1 You**: probably Emily Sellwood. **96, 5 one**: Hallam. **96, 22–4 Sinai's peaks . . . trumpet**: cf. Exodus xix.16. The trumpet heralded the presence of God on Mt Sinaï, when Moses received the Ten Commandments. **100–1** These poems refer to Tennyson's move from Somersby in 1837. **101, 11 the lesser wain**: the Little Bear (a constellation). **105** The third of three lyrics marking the passing of Christmas (the others are numbers 30 and 78). Together they give a sense of sequence to the poem as a whole. Here Tennyson imagines transcending the rituals of the past (105), and welcoming the future (106). **105, 5 father's dust**: Tennyson's father had died six years before the family left Somersby. **105, 25 rising worlds**: stars or planets. **106, 32 the Christ that is to be**: 'The broader Christianity of the future' (Tennyson). **115, 2 quick**: 'quickset thorn' (Tennyson). **117, 9–12** time measured by hour-glass, sundial, clock and the movements of the stars. **123, 1–8** geological change, reflecting Tennyson's reading of Lyell.

From *Ode on the Death of the Duke of Wellington* Published November 1852, two days before Wellington's state funeral. Tennyson wrote the poem because he thought it was expected of him as Poet Laureate. Wellington, Britain's military hero during the Napoleonic Wars and victor at Waterloo, had subsequently been a Tory Prime Minister (1828–30). Earlier in 1852 Tennyson had written a number of patriotic songs in response to public fear of invasion by France after the *coup d'état* of Louis Napoleon. **9 roar**: Wellington was buried in St Paul's Cathedral. **197 horn**: Fortune is depicted with the horn of plenty (cornucopia). **229 iron**: Wellington was known as the 'Iron Duke', a reference to his strength of will. **259 Giant Ages**: geological forces working over long periods.

The Charge of the Light Brigade Written and published in December 1854 after reading a report in *The Times* about this event in the Crimean War.

From *Maud: A Monodrama* (*1855* – revised for *1856*; later divided into parts) See Introduction. The protagonist broods on the disinheritance and suicide of his father, blaming the man who inherited the family wealth. He notes with suspicion the return of the inheritor's daughter, Maud, whom he knew in childhood and to whom her father and his own father had planned an engagement. Gradually acknowledging his feeling for her, he develops a hatred of her brother and of the suitor he brings, the heir of a mine-owner. Maud returns his love, but her brother insults him and a duel is fought in which the brother dies, acknowledging, however, that 'the fault was mine' (beginning of Part 2). Maud is distraught and soon dies too, and the protagonist, tormented by her image and his guilt, first experiences the illusion that he too is dead, and then enlists as a soldier in the Crimean War.

Part 1
1, 2 blood-red: Tennyson considered the extravagance of the phrase an early sign of the speaker's madness. **1, 21 blessings of Peace**: nearly forty years after Warterloo there was a widespread feeling that pacifism was merely a cloak for money-making interests, and that Britain *needed* a war. This is generally counted as one of the causes of the Crimean War (1854–6). **1, 35 ledger lives**: life is ruled by financial calculation. **1, 37 vitriol**: sulphuric acid, used in the adulteration of tea. **1, 39 for bread**: adulteration of bread was notorious in the early 1850s. **1, 41 centre-bits**: instruments for boring holes; here used by burglars. **1, 44 poison**: drugs (often opium derivatives) recklessly dispensed by the chemist. **1, 45 burial fee**: poor parents could make regular payments into a 'burial society' to cover the cost if their children died. Some killed their children to collect the money. **1, 46 Timour-Mammon**: Timur the Lame (1336–1405), Turkish conqueror; Mammon, wealth regarded as a god. **10, 37–45** Interpreted at the time as an attack on John Bright, MP, who represented the cotton interests and was a Quaker. **10, 41 broad-brimm'd**: referring to the type of hat worn at one time by Quakers. **10, 65 Aristocrat**: accented on the second syllable, as was usual at the time. **22, 8 planet of Love**: Venus, the morning star.

Part 2
1, 1 The fault was mine: the words of Maud's brother after he has been shot. **1, 5 a passionate cry**: Maud's at the sight of the bloodshed; this and the following lines echo God's words to Cain after he had killed Abel (Genesis iv. 10–11). **1, 27 Christless code**: revenge. **4** Written in 1833–4 and published in 1837. When it became the nucleus of *Maud*, it was further revised. **4, 11 shadow**: a projection of the hero's guilt in the form of a

'phantom' of Maud as she appeared at the moment of uttering her 'cry for a brother's blood' (2, 1, 34). This 'phantom' is distinct from the 'happy spirit' (2, 4, 81) of the Maud who accepted the hero as her lover. **5, 18 the dead men**: the other inmates of the asylum. **5, 22 bury a man**: possibly a reference to frequent abuses in funerals of the poor, such as overcrowding, the use of mass graves and the sale of bodies for dissection. **5, 28–9** A reference to divisions within the Anglican Church in the 1840s and 1850s, the period of the Oxford Movement and the Evangelicals. Many Anglicans felt threatened by the re-establishment of a Roman Catholic hierarchy in Britain in 1850. **5, 53 gray old wolf**: Maud's father. **5, 58–9** The protagonist associates Hanoverian ancestry with the introduction into England of the brown Norwegian rat: a Jacobite claim after the Hanoverian succession in 1714. **5, 63 poison our babes**: recalling the social evils denounced in 1, 1, 37–46. **5, 80 a dead man**: himself, as he imagines. **5, 82 Sultan**: Maud's brother. **5, 85 a friend of mine**: the hero's father. **5, 88 the second corpse**: Maud's brother. **5, 92 the Quaker**: the protagonist thinks of his shooting of Maud's brother as a blow struck at a public enemy, in a just war.

Part 3
'Sane, but shattered. Written when the cannon was heard booming from the battleships in the Solent before the Crimean War' (Tennyson). The numeral '6' is a relic of an earlier version of the poem when this section was the sixth and last lyric of Part 2: the text given here is the whole of Part 3, the final part of the poem. **6, 6–8 Charioteer . . . Gemini**: constellations. The season is evidently spring. **6, 10 She**: the true spirit of Maud as distinct from the 'phantom'. **6, 13–14 Mars . . . on the Lion's breast**: the planet Mars stands for war; the constellation Leo (lion) for Britain. **6, 20 iron tyranny**: Czarist Russia. **6, 34 deck**: of a troopship bound for the Crimea. **6, 36 phantom**: Maud. **6, 45 giant liar**: Czar Nicholas I. Many in Britain regarded as hypocritical Russia's claim to be fighting a holy war in Turkey. **6, 51 the Black and the Baltic**: two seas where British naval power engaged Russian forces.

Tithonus (*1860*) Written in a shorter form following Hallam's death, as a 'pendant' to 'Ulysses'. Tithonus was loved by Aurora, goddess of the dawn, who gave him immortality but not eternal youth. Though he grew old and shrunken, he could not die; nor could she take back the gift. **4 swan**: noted for its long life and the fact that it sings only as death approaches. **6 thine arms**: Aurora's. **25 the silver star**: Venus, the morning star. **30 goal of

ordinance: appointed limit. **39 team**: the horses which draw Aurora's chariot daily from Ocean to Olympus. **50 with what another heart**: with how different feelings. **62 Apollo**: the god of wisdom and poetry, to whose music Troy (Ilion) arose.

Northern Farmer – New Style (*1869*) One of a number of poems in which Tennyson used Lincolnshire dialect. He supplied some of the glosses below. **1 'erse's**: horse's. **4 nor**: than. **5 Woä**: stop; **a craw to pluck wi' tha**: something to settle with you. **7 to weeäk**: this week. **8 mysén**: myself. **17 stunt**: obstinate. **26 addle**: earn. **27 hissen**: himself. **28 ligs**: lies. **32 far-welter'd**: fow-weltered (said of a sheep lying on its back). **39 mays nowt**: makes nothing. **40 the bees is as fell as owt**: the flies are as fierce as anything. **41 esh**: ashwood. **49 mun 'a**: must have. **52 tued an' moil'd**: worked and slaved. **55 brig**: bridge. (The farmer is pointing out the extent of his land.)

From *Merlin and Vivien* First published in 1859 as *Vivien* and subsequently part of *Idylls of the King* (see Introduction). **178 fits**: moods. **187–94** Merlin foresees the destruction of the Round Table. **202 Broceliande**: an enchanted forest in Brittany. **247 elf-god eyeless**: Cupid (love), imagined as blind. **248 arras hall**: hall hung with tapestries.

To E. FitzGerald (*1885*) Edward FitzGerald, translator of *The Rubáiyát of Omar Khayyám* (1859) and an old friend of Tennyson, died in 1883 just after this poem was finished. **1 suburb grange**: FitzGerald's home, Little Grange, Woodbridge, Suffolk. **11 that full sheet**: see Acts x.11–14, telling of St Peter's unwillingness, when hungry, to eat food unless God specifically allowed it. **15 table of Pythagoras**: vegetarian diet: Pythagoras believed human souls could inhabit animals. **17 has it**: in *Measure for Measure*, I, iv. **28 Eshcol**: a river: having cut a bunch of grapes there, the Israelites named it Eshcol, meaning 'bunch of grapes'. See Numbers xiii.23–4. **32 golden Eastern lay**: the *Rubáiyát*. **40 Old friends**: James Spedding and W. H. Brookfield. **46 my son**: Hallam Tennyson. **50 this**: 'Tiresias', a poem appended to this one in 1885.

Crossing the Bar (*1889*) Tennyson said that he 'began and finished' this lyric in twenty minutes and wished it to appear at the end of all editions of his poems. A 'bar' is a bank of sand or silt across the mouth of a river or harbour. **3 moaning**: the sound of the sea in bad weather. **13 bourne**: boundary, limit.

June Bracken and Heather (*1892*) Addressed to Tennyson's wife Emily; summer 1891.

Help us make the next generation of readers

We – both author and publisher – hope you enjoyed this book. We believe that you can become a reader at any time in your life, but we'd love your help to give the next generation a head start.

Did you know that 9 per cent of children don't have a book of their own in their home, rising to 13 per cent in disadvantaged families*? We'd like to try to change that by asking you to consider the role you could play in helping to build readers of the future.

We'd love you to think of sharing, borrowing, reading, buying or talking about a book with a child in your life and spreading the love of reading. We want to make sure the next generation continue to have access to books, wherever they come from.

And if you would like to consider donating to charities that help fund literacy projects, find out more at **www.literacytrust.org.uk** and **www.booktrust.org.uk**.

THANK YOU

*As reported by the National Literacy Trust